THE MAKING OF NEW CULTURES

NEW SERIES   VOLUME XXXIV

COSTERUS

AMSTERDAM 1982

THE MAKING OF NEW CULTURES

A Literary Perspective

By
Colin Partridge

To
The University of Victoria,
British Columbia, Canada
and
The Flinders University
of South Australia

It is true that no particularism can adequately incarnate the good. But is it not also true that only through some particular roots, however partial, can human beings first grasp what is good and it is the juice of such roots which for most men sustain their partaking in a more universal good?

George Grant, *Technology and Empire*

ACKNOWLEDGEMENTS

The extract from the work of Don Gutteridge is reprinted from *A True History of Lambton County* by permission of Oberon Press, Ottawa.

CONTENTS

Chapter One

THE MYSTERY OF CULTURE

*Lord, when shall we be done growing? As
long as we have anything more to do, we have
done nothing.*
Melville to Hawthorne, November 1851

(1)

Culture is humanity's fabricated environment; it is human-kind's grandest invention within which social structure, individual relations, art and religion take substance, meaning and form.

Emerging from a particular place and developing through measurable time, a culture represents an original system of values between persons and a geophysical reality. It is a defined series of active meanings that helps people adapt to change by evoking the past and anticipating the future.

In its beginnings a culture reveals and structures varying human responses to basic necessity; it establishes patterns which help in providing material subsistence, dividing the responsibilities of procreation, transmitting attitudes and duties to the next generation, and accepting the unwelcome incursions of accident, sickness and death. The public attitudes and behavioral patterns responding to such realities give rise to specific and arbitrary values which, becoming more defined in time, form a system that influences personal and collective behavior.

A culture's value-system is often represented by carefully selected symbols, some of which are lodged, as in a protective sheath, within narratives; these oral or written texts, of mythic or pseudo-historical epic nature, dramatize the group's defined responses to necessity. The resolutions to conflicts between protagonists and adversaries clarify and endorse identifiable values central to the evolving system. Basic values, therefore, tend to become con-

gealed in narratives which, if repeated with sufficient fervor, especially to the young, take on the aura of truth and become incorporated into the modes of perception by which successive generations
view necessity.

The triumph of a culture is the incorporation of its values
into the processes of perception. The emotional, mental and phys-
iological responses of individuals and groups are then to a large
extent predetermined by the culture's values. Resolute dissidents
may protest, but they can never fully evade the cultural processes
which are locked into their very beings and into their human language. What began as flexible responses essential for personal and
collective survival in the face of necessity coagulate through time
into a predetermined mode of viewing reality. Professional guard-
ians appoint themselves to jealously protect the original narratives,
sometimes regarded as "sacred" or products of some prior "revela-
tion"; to challenge their predetermined worth, original accuracy or
contemporary relevance may be hazardous, as the fate of heretics in
diverse societies through the ages pathetically demonstrates. On the
other hand, accepting the once arbitrary but now congealed values
tends to limit behavior within commonly agreed, or controlled,
structures; the freedoms of flexible experiment, fundamental dis-
sent and behavioral disobedience are diminished or lost. Thus in
defining responses to basic necessity, in clarifying values and making a culture, the possibilities of personal and group security have
been increased; but the price paid in time is a built-in perceptual
bias which may limit the freedom of divergent mental or social
behavior.

There were eras when all cultures were new. But by the late
twentieth century some had become solidified in their own biases,
unable or unwilling to adapt to innovations embodied in other
value-systems; they became subordinate to innovative cultures
which, in times of improved communications, tend to dominate.
This subordination of traditional, established cultures happened
not only in many Asian and African countries but also in much of
Europe.

There are other cultures which, conscious of their sterile inequitable values in a twentieth-century world, have attempted to renovate their antiquated structures by social revolution; the most notable instances are the Soviet Union and the People's Republic of China.

However, in contrast to both subordinate and self-renewing value-systems, there exist other cultures — some demonstrating immense innovative energy — that are still relatively new on the global scene, having been born only within the past five hundred years.

(2)

This crucial period in human affairs has been characterized by the rise and fall of European value-systems. A primary consequence of Europe's past technological and economic hegemony was the founding of new societies. These colonies, scattered around the world, were at first the passive recipients of expansionist European technology and administration. They received the founding nation's language together with the established values and modes of perception enclosed in the language.

But the new societies of North and South America, the Caribbean and the South Pacific confronted new forms of necessity; the survival and security of people living in an alien and initially hostile terrain, as well as accommodation to the mother country's culture and economic power, demanded unconventional or innovative responses. In experiencing these and establishing social patterns distinctive to the geophysical reality, the inhabitants of new societies discovered that the values which were imported or imposed never exactly fitted their responses to necessity. They began to modify European cultures and clarify their innovative responses to life and growth in the new land. The conscious process of making new cultures was under way.

Four major formative experiences contribute to the making of a new culture:

1. Scrutiny of imported values, especially those from the dominant

founding culture, and continuing attempts to select those values thought appropriate for retention

2. Formulation of original responses to the unknown, initially threatening, land

3. Attempts at a later period, after successive waves of immigration, to reconcile the different sub-cultures of the different immigrant groups (biculturalism or multiculturalism)

4. Belated recognition that the indigenous population before European dominance had shaped a viable culture from which people in the present might extract values to invest in their multicultural society.

The making of new cultures and the development of technology are the most sustained achievements of recent centuries. Not only have complex societies been formed but also mental processes have been inaugurated that were not part of former old-world consciousness. The making of new cultures has created new insights into both human relationships and humanity's relationship with necessity. The study of their formation shows the shaping of human values and their incorporation into modes of perception. Literary texts massively document and dramatize this complex achievement.

All new cultures developed when Romantic assumptions held sway in Europe and when the influence of Romanticism was inescapable in the European dependencies. Large importance was attached to the role of artist, and especially the literary artist; this person of imagination in the new society played a key role in surveying the culture's needs, shaping new attitudes and restructuring the imported European language. In the United States this key role was performed by such different writers as Walt Whitman , Mark Twain, Robert Frost, Sherwood Anderson and William Faulkner.

More recently, in South America, writers such as Pablo Neruda, Gabriel García Márquez, Carlos Fuentes and Mario Vargas

Llosa have performed a similar task: to express their South American experience they surveyed the European influences that contributed to it, their culture's development over the centuries and, like their North American counterparts, contrived new structures of narrative and language.

All new societies are multiethnic. This fact necessitates complex social responses that shape the culture's formation. There are many varieties of multiethnic diversity. In some societies, as in the Quechua-speaking Andean countries, the original non-European inhabitants may comprise the majority of the population. Other societies are characterized by a value-system deriving mainly from Europe, although a significant number of the population are descended from African-born slaves, as in many Caribbean islands. Other societies show ethnic division between successive waves of immigration with different sub-groups hovering on the verge of open conflict.

To achieve cultural integration it is usually necessary to overcome the prejudice that a sub-group has nothing to contribute to the emerging whole. There is a need to assert that all groups have some values worthy of incorporation and preservation. To such a task the Peruvian writer José María Arguedas dedicated his life as poet, novelist and ethnographer. He sought to reveal in his work, expressed in a restructured Spanish, the values of Quechua culture which the politically dominant Spanish-based elite in Peru had despised or rejected for centuries.

Arguedas' utterances were conscious efforts to reveal a suppressed portion of Peruvian culture. Comparable to this is the work of the Barbadian poet and historian Edward Brathwaite; after training as a historian in England, researching the black slave life of the Caribbean plantations, he journeyed to Ghana in order to explore the Akan culture from which the slaves had been wrested. Brathwaite understood that Caribbean society could evolve only by identifying, acknowledging and incorporating values that shaped the lives of large segments of the population. To remove from them the taint of inferiority, he sought understanding at their African source before returning to the Caribbean to celebrate their vitality.

Another Caribbean writer, the novelist and journalist V.S. Naipaul, travelled to India to understand the values of the society from which his forebears had come; he also sought a cultural source for attitudes and customs characterizing the East Indian communities in which he had grown up in ethnically divided Trinidad. He later lived in Europe, Africa and South America to appreciate better the values shaping the Caribbean islands.

A writer more subtly aware of the problems of multiethnic integration is Wilson Harris. Coming from Guyana with its mixed Amerindian, Dutch, British, African, Chinese and East Indian population, he has attempted to dramatize in his fiction the different values of the different sub-groups. Conscious always of the fearful ravages of racial conflict, Harris has warned of the possible "collisions of culture" and advocated a humane, creative tolerance in which the integrated psyche represents the integrated healthy culture.

(3)

Given these problems of social integration and the contradictions of sub-group diversity it is not surprising that the literatures of new cultures dramatize concerns different from those of older cultures. A general characteristic of new cultures is a concern with analyzing both the origins of the culture and the processes that formed the value-system. These analyses reach to the root assumptions of the society's being and tend to dramatize four main areas of social experience in the culture's formation:

1. Evocation of original explorations, early contacts with the unfamiliar terrain, and the bestowal of names

2. Evocations of journeys which explored or opened to settlement the interior of the territory

3. Radical analysis of established patterns of family structure

4. Radical analysis of established patterns of socio-political structure.

Many artists from new societies exist with an inalienable sense of their culture's restless growth. They know their origins are not comfortably obscured in prehistorical mists but belong to a precise, mathematical time; they know the processes of cultural change have been recorded with the fine lasting detail that characterizes the ages of print when their societies were born; so for sensitive artists both contemporary reality and an entire evolution suggest restless growth which requires continued radical analysis. There is a sense in which new-world writers of the nineteenth and early twentieth centuries, conscious of their cultures' recent beginnings and developmental struggles, anticipated the anxiety of later twentieth-century artists from older cultures who urged the reexamination of coagulated values in an effort to renew primal vision. Generally, artists from new cultures cannot escape the brilliance or the anguish of primal vision. When they look around, especially after experiencing an older civilization, everything in their own culture seems too fresh, too stark. The imminence of origins is inescapable, the need to examine them patently obvious; and the processes that shaped the culture are so recent that responsibility for deficiencies can still be assigned and remedial actions insistently advocated. This distinctive combination of attitudes, analyses and advocacies is evident in the work of the Australian writer Patrick White.

When he returned to Australia after a long residence in Europe, White committed himself to writing about his new-world society. He soon experienced the starkness of seeing in a fresh way:

> So I began to write *The Tree of Man* . . . Writing, which had meant the practice of an art by a polished mind in civilized surroundings, became a struggle to create completely fresh

forms out of the rocks and sticks of words. I began to see things for the first time. Even the boredom and frustration presented avenues for endless exploration; even the ugliness, the bags and iron of Australian life, acquired a meaning.[1]

The "fresh forms" soon required the fashioning of new linguistic structures and the variety of Australian life necessitated analysis of its formation and established patterns. Over the next twenty years, in novel after novel, White dramatized different aspects of the culture's formation. *The Tree of Man* (1956) detailed a family's domestication of the wilderness; *Voss* (1958) contrasted mannered Sydney society of the 1830s with exploration of the unknown continent looming behind the tiny settlement; *Riders in the Chariot* (1961) dramatized the distance separating outsiders or social misfits from conventionally accepted lifestyles; *The Eye of the Storm* (1970) was White's version of the International Theme showing the uneasy contrast of Australian and European values; *A Fringe of Leaves* (1976) ironically compared the power of mannered colonial society with the power necessary to survive in the outback. All these types of experience had been previously presented in other narratives by other Australian writers; but White's social and psychological perceptiveness, technical skill and verbal brilliance gave new insights into the making of Australian culture.

(4)

This concern with origin and process in cultural formation that is characteristic of White and other major writers from new societies is finely evoked by the Anglophone Canadian writer Don Gutteridge in his verse narrative *A True History of Lambton County* (1977). A narrator, standing firmly in the present, contemplates a piece of farmland; his mind ranges back to the place's origins and its accretions of experience through time; the transformation of the land from bush to farm, which is also White's cultural theme in *The*

Tree of Man, preoccupies him and leads to a statement about the crucial stages of making a new cultural expression. The narrator imagines the words of a figure like Stan Parker, the first pioneer in the area:

> It's nouns we need:
> ancient bone-words
> we Christen each
> farm with chart
> the unnameable doubt
>
> Later on, there'll be
> room for the bloodbeat of verbs,
> the fancy-flesh
> adjective, the river
> of our sentence complete
> (though mine be the chatty and backtracking
> hopelessly local
> Aux Saubles)
>
> And farther still:
> beyond the first city
> first green century —
> the luxury of
> myth and metaphor . . .
>
> Meantime, this axe-blow
> I utter on wood may
> yet kindle the magic noun,
> the home-made legend
> no grandson of the second
> century can doubt.[2]

The structuring grammatical metaphor reminds us of the two essential aspects of making a culture: transforming the land to ensure material subsistence and achieving self-articulation — that is, making a poetry of sound, line and movement which helps to clarify human relationship with the new environment.

The first need is to name: in Gutteridge's evocation, the bestowal of names is comparable to the axe-blow of the pioneer in the silent forest; it is not a merely practical act but possesses also a spiritual function akin to the magical connection established by tribal societies between the "maker" and the "made". The unknown becomes less dauntingly dominant by familiarizing it with a name of one's choosing; in the raw unknown landscape it demarcates an area of known certainty shaped by the newcomers' labours and contrasts with the larger uncertainty of the unknown terrain.

Only after naming does measurable satisfying action become possible. The original proper noun is succeeded by verbs, adjectives, syntactical structures representative not only of settlement and domestication but also of the increasingly complex ties that develop with residence through several generations in one place. The newcomers have survived; and basic necessity is slowly replaced by varieties of needs requiring more subtle expressions of language and thought.

A still later stage in this complexifying process is the making of myth and metaphor — the "home-made legend" through which later inhabitants will view the place's origin and development. By this time factual history has been succeeded in general consciousness by poetic or mythic history. The new culture now shapes people's perceptions of the past; the original raw reality is enfolded in levels of non-factual narrative that reveal the culture's conscious development.

It is a process of accretion very similar to that dramatized by William Carlos Williams in the five books of *Paterson*. Amid the mass of twentieth-century banality the town of Paterson has lost its founding magic of settlement. But in a manner characteristic of writers from new cultures Williams asserts that rediscovery and renewal are possible by exposing the place's social origins and examin-

ing the processes of its cultural formation. The force accompanying
this is the power of imaginative invention:

> Without invention nothing is well spaced,
> unless the mind change, unless
> the stars are new measured, according
> to their relative positions the
> line will not change, the necessity
> will not matriculate.[3]

Invention, which is comparable to the Romantic concept of Imagination, produces new measurements. Williams, whose view of new
cultures extended beyond the United States to South America and
the Caribbean, understood that making adequate responses to new
geophysical reality demanded changes of perspective. New-world
necessity required new measurements. Consciousness had to
change if people were to survive; apparent fixities and absolutes
had to be abandoned; only immersion in process could reveal the
patterns of the new.

This emphasis upon process to uncover origins and cultural
formation is evident in comparable works such as Walt Whitman's
Song of Myself, Aimé Césaire's *Journal d'un retour au pays natal*, Pablo
Neruda's *Canto general* and Edward Brathwaite's *The Arrivants: A
New World Trilogy*. In these complex evocative works the writer's
function is akin to that of the pioneer. He binds himself to a place
and a posture; he names, performs actions, and makes patterns of
relationship within that place; his imaginative invention integrates
words, sentences and metaphors into a "home-made legend." His
progression from naming to myth-making contributes to forming
an original system of values. The pioneer's major efforts, confronting necessity, transformed geophysical reality; the post-Romantic,
pioneering artist's efforts were continually shaping series of active,
non-material meanings that enabled people to adapt to the continuing necessity of making minute changes in private and public life —

or, in the phrase of the American poet Wallace Stevens, to making his imagination light in the mind of others.

Gutteridge's poem offers useful classifications for surveying the stages of social and artistic development in new cultures.

The first imaginative response to the unknown land is the bestowal of bone-words, or names, by navigators, inland explorers, christianizing missionaries, first settlers and colonial administrators. The beginning of a new culture is the act of naming places; the beginning of the new literature is the record of these acts in log-books, journals and official accounts of exploration and settlement.

Later comes the "bloodbeat of verbs" when settlers reshape the land by acting on established values within the named boundaries. The new literature often presents contemporary experiences of settlement in writing as rugged as the stubborn soil first turned by the pioneer's plough. Melodramatic description, journalistic cliches and literary conventions from old-world literatures often characterize first accounts of shaping the environment. The work of Frederick Philip Grove in Canada, Alexander Harris in Australia, William Satchell in New Zealand, Rómulo Gallegos, Ciro Alegría and Ricardo Güiraldes in South America typify this stage of literary dramatization in making a new cultural awareness.

The third stage is when experiences emerge from an increasingly complex social structure and are presented in complex formulations; this stage depends on an accomplished possession by an accomplished artist of the new culture's unique experiences. The works enclose a culture's past and present but, unlike journalistic or documentary reportage, they are constructed to offer diverse meanings on symbolic, mythic or iconographic levels. The "home-made" legends are, in fact, extremely sophisticated achievements and are the points at which the international reader usually encounters the literary productions of new societies. This crucial stage is represented by major works such as Hawthorne's *The Scarlet Letter* (1850), Whitman's *Song of Myself* (1855), Ringuet's *Trente Arpents* (1938), Aimé Césaire's *Journal d'un retour au pays natal* (1938),

Miguel Ángel Asturias' *Hombres de maiz* (1949), Pablo Neruda's *Canto general* (1950), Juan Rulfo's *Pedro Páramo* (1953), Patrick White's *The Tree of Man* (1956) and Alejo Carpentier's *El siglo de las luces* (1962). These are works in which the author's mediating vision coalesces with socio-historical reality. So powerful is the vision, so assured his linguistic and formal skills that the artist's imaginative interpretation lodges itself as light in the mind of others and contributes to the making of a unique cultural perception.

The final stage in establishing a new culture, which often coincides with the shaping of home-made legends, is acceptance of — and pride in — the resources of local language. New cultures originally received matured language systems from European sources. But in time, under the pressures of new necessities, the colloquial languages took on structures and vocabularies different from their European origins. Although grammarians, basing their usage on the leisurely utterances of ruling classes in the old countries, offered prescriptive rules to regulate deviant practice, some imp of the perverse exercised its linguistic will in the new territories. The energy of colloquial discourse flooded the dams of old-world standardized usage. This gave many writers a chance to choose: they could express themselves in the orthodox structures of the mother country's language; they could explore the possibilities of their own culture's colloquial usage; or they could fashion an amalgam drawn from old-world orthodoxy and new regional inventiveness. The decision to experiment the better to express their vision of the developing culture was made by writers as different as Mark Twain, Sherwood Anderson and William Faulkner in the United States; Joseph Furphy and Patrick White in Australia; Margaret Laurence and Alice Monro in Anglophone Canada; Ringuet in Francophone Canada; Miguel Ángel Asturias, José María Arguedas and João Guimarães Rosa in different South American countries.

A distinctive consequence follows upon a major writer's successful use of colloquial resources. He reveals to others — both fellow artists and reading-public — the possible strengths of local ex-

pression. He shows that regional linguistic innovation is no longer a barbarism to be avoided in favour of established old-world rules; instead it may convey a fuller sense of the culture's presence and its inhabitants' consciousness than the formalities of conventional utterance. Not even Henry James could remain unaware of Mark Twain, or A.D. Hope of Patrick White.

But some innovators have grave doubts about using the colloquial. Gaston Panneton, who wrote in Quebec under the pen-name Ringuet, thought long and carefully about employing rural Quebec dialect in his fiction. There had been times as a young man visiting Europe when he felt embarrassed by his linguistic inheritance. But in middle life, when he came to write his masterpiece *Trente arpents* he found there was no way to present the traditional life-style of Quebec *habitants* except by reproducing *habitant* speech patterns. *Trente arpents* begins:

—On va commencer betôt les guérêts, m'sieu Branchaud. Mon oncle m'a dit comme ça en partant: I'faudra labourer le champ en bas de la côte, demain. Si seulement y peut s'arrêter de mouiller!

Les deux hommes se turent. Assis sur leurs chaises accotées contre le mur, en équilibre sur deux pieds, à intervalles égaux ils retiraient leur pipe et, se penchant hors de la véranda, lançaient dans les herbes folles un jet de salive. Puis ils reprenaient leur calme posture, les yeux perdus.

Autour d'eux s'étalait la Plaine que les premières gelées d'octobre avaient peinte de couleurs vives. Des boqueteaux tiraient l'oeil, les saules noirs déjà nus brochant sur les hêtres encore verts.[4]

"We've got to start in on the ploughing now that autumn's on us, m'sieu Branchaud. The last thing my uncle said to me, just as he was leaving: 'Tomorrow we got to plough up that field at the foot of the hill.' If only this pouring rain would rest up awhiles."

The two men became silent. Seated on chairs tilted against the wall, balanced on two legs, they took their pipes from their mouths at regular intervals and, leaning forward over the veranda, spat expertly into the lank grass. Then they resumed their peaceful pose, their eyes absorbed in the long land.

All around them stretched the Laurentian Plain that the first October frosts had painted with vivid colours. Clumps of trees attracted their eyes; the black willows were already leafless forming a pattern with the still green beeches.[5]

The opening paragraph of dialect establishes the living connection between people and soil. The vocabulary and phrasing convey the speakers' oneness with the land but suggest also their farmerlike reverence and exasperation for the earth on which they depend.

In his second paragraph Ringuet uses an orthodox vocabulary and firm sentence structure that could have been composed by Flaubert. It subtly reinforces the opening impressions by suggesting a timeless ritual in the posture and tiny movements of the two men. Ringuet's images flow one into another, as the habitants' gaze absorb the land, and the land absorbs their lifelong labours.

A comparable masterpiece, another novel dramatizing the relationships of persons with new-world soil, is Patrick White's *The Tree of Man*. It begins:

A cart drove between the two big stringybarks and stopped. These were the dominant trees in that part of the bush, rising above the involved scrub with the simplicity of true grandeur. So the cart stopped, grazing the hairy side of a tree, and the horse, shaggy and stolid as the tree, sighed and took root.

The man who sat in the cart got down. He rubbed his hands together, because already it was cold . . . Birds looked

from twigs, and the eyes of animals were drawn to what was
happening. The man lifting a bundle from a cart. A dog
lifting his leg on an anthill. The lip drooping on the sweaty
horse.[6]

Like Ringuet, White uses conventional third-person narration for
the poetic-realist novel but, unlike him, White dislocates his images
of the landscape. He separates them so that they become like a series
of still frames in a film sequence. The fractured sentences, which
form a minor climax at the end of the second paragraph, are terse
colloquial formulations that reinforce the effect conveyed by the
taut natural images; together they suggest isolation, courage,
genesis.

Ringuet's language, syntax and use of imagery in *Trent
arpents* imply centuries-long continuity of life on the Quebec land;
White's language, syntax and dislocated imagery in *The Tree of Man*
suggest the starkness of a first beginning. Each novelist draws upon
the resources of colloquial speech to express the reality of life in the
new environment.

Often a writer may convey a greater sense of immediacy to
consciousness and culture by employing first-person narration.
This tends to make his raid upon colloquial resources even vaster;
his art requires finer selection of material and the greatest linguistic
subtlety. Two of the most skilful users of first-person innovative col-
loquialism are the New Zealand fiction writer Frank Sargeson and
the Brazilian writer João Guimarães Rosa.

Sargeson's novella *That Summer* begins by evoking a consciousness dissatisfied with its rural surroundings:

It was a good farm job I had that winter, but I've always
suffered from itchy feet so I never thought I'd stick it for
long. All the same I stayed until the shearing, and I quit
after we'd carted the wool out to the station, just a few bales
at a time. It was just beginning December and I had a good

lot of chips saved up, so I thought I'd have a spell in town which I hadn't had for a' good long time, and maybe I'd strike a town job before my chips ran out.[7]

The sentence structure, which is a series of assertions followed by qualifications, offers an insight into self-justifying behavior. "It was . . . but . . . so . . . All the same . . . " These simple transitional words signify a pattern of emotional and intellectual response that exactly portrays a type of wandering New Zealander. The colloquial movement of private assertion and qualification suggests a rapid alternation between independence and subordination characterizing a whole cultural attitude. Sargeson's art is revealed by his accurate choice of commonplace words and the subtle balance of colloquial phrase; they combine to dramatize a consciousness and a culture.

João Guimarães Rosa's great epic of Brazil, *Grande Sertão: Veredas*, begins with uncompromising colloquial assertiveness:

Nonada. Tiros que o senhor ouviu foram de briga de homen não, Deus esteja. Alvejei mira em árvore, no quintal, no baixo do córrego. Por meu acêrto. Todo dia isso faco, gosto; desde mal en minha mocedade.[8]

Nothing. The shots you heard, sir, weren't men brawling, praise God. I was just shooting at a tree, in the orchard, down by the creek. Improving my aim. Every day I do it — and enjoy it — from the bad things I did in my youth.

Guimarães Rosa's use of the colloquial is initially disconcerting. It disrupts a reader's linguistic expectations, whereas Sargeson's usage tends *almost* to fulfil a reader's anticipations of words and phrases. In Guimarães Rosa's work one can never anticipate the next phrase or word. His intent is to invent a whole new world, so the language is fresh-minted. In the beginning is nothingness, then comes the sound of the first shots. Riobaldo the narrator will ponder his position in a world of ritual violence. As a maker of that world, he has a god-like capability which is evidenced by his linguistic inventiveness. But he lives unsure about the existence of an opposing power — one that is evil or diabolical. Guimarães Rosa's novel ponders this traditional metaphysical obsession in a distinctively Brazilian context by forcing the boundaries of the colloquial Brazilian language; his words and structures defy conventional syntax, just as the actions of his characters outrage conventional behaviour.

These are a few instances of accomplished writers' diverse assaults upon the old-world structures of new-world languages. The linguistic necessity they faced, while different in type from that confronting their settler-forebears, required similar innovative resourcefulness to articulate the new environment: the settlers' reality had been primarily geophysical; the artists' reality was both material and non-material; their successful Invention, in Williams' sense, like the invention of the cotton-gin or combine-harvester that transformed patterns of work, profoundly affected the new culture's self-definition.

(5)

Perhaps the ideal condition for the linguistic maturation of a new culture is when two or more different, but separate, continuing experiments take place to change established structures. This has occurred most consistently in the United States. Mark Twain's inheritance of written and spoken frontier speech produced one of the most distinctive beginnings to any novel in world literature. *The Adventures of Huckleberry Finn* begins:

> You don't know about me without you have read a book by the name of *The Adventures of Tom Sawyer*, but that ain't no matter.

The self-assurance, the directness of address, the outsider posture

and the extraordinary rhythms structuring this verbal aggressive-
ness contribute to a remarkable self-definition in United States' culture. The distance between this and Charles Dickens' first-person
narrators represents an unbridgeable gulf. *The Adventures of Huckleberry Finn* was first published in 1884. Twenty-four years previously
Dickens had started *Great Expectations* with the words:

> My father's family name being Pirrip, and my christian
> name Philip, my infant tongue could make of both names
> nothing longer or more explicit than Pip.

Twenty-one years before composing *Great Expectations*, he had
started *David Copperfield*:

> Whether I shall turn out to be the hero of my own life, or
> whether that station will be held by anybody else, these
> pages must show.

The English narrators' propriety and the linguistic structure Dickens used to enclose their social orthodoxy reveal differences not
merely of character and situation but of irrevocably diverging
cultures.

A generation after the publication of *Huckleberry Finn* a second assault upon conventional structures came from a number of
midwestern American writers. A major figure is Sherwood Ander-
soon. He influenced Ernest Hemingway whose style was also shaped
by contemporary journalism as much as by the linguistic innovations of Gertrude Stein. When Hemingway describes a landscape
there is no doubt from which culture the description derives.

> There was no town, nothing but the rails and the burned-
> over country. The thirteen saloons that had lined the one
> street of Seney had not left a trace. The foundations of the
> Mansion House hotel stuck up above the ground. The stone

was chipped and split by the fire. It was all that was left of
the town of Seney. Even the surface had been burned off
the ground.[9]

The terse colloquial rhythm is unyielding as it grates on a reader's
nerves. The diverse details are carefully selected so as to establish
one perspective. Then the taut language contrives a tension between the camera-eye diversity of details and the singleness of the
perspective. The simple vocabulary, any word of which could be
heard in a small-town bar, conceals a web of implications, the full
meaning of which goes far beyond bar-room story-telling.

In the 1920s and 1930s a third linguistic innovator was William Faulkner. Like Hemingway he was influenced to some degree
by Sherwood Anderson's conscious Americanizing of rhythms and
his use of deceptively simple language; but Faulkner also inherited
a style of inflated political-evangelical rhetoric pervasive in the
American South. His merging of the two distinguishes his unique
Southern expression:

> Behind the smokehouse that summer, Ringo and I had a
> living map. Although Vicksburg was just a handful of chips
> from the woodpile and the River a trench scraped into the
> packed earth with the point of a hoe, it (river, city, and ter-
> rain) lived, possessing even in miniature that ponderable
> though passive recalcitrance of topography which out-
> weighs artillery, against which the most brilliant of victories
> and the most tragic of defeats are but the loud noises of a
> moment.[10]

The colloquial nostalgic familiarity of the opening sentence soon
gives way to a complex Latinate structure in which the sharp images
contrast with abstract concepts and implied paradoxes. Faulkner's
rhythms suggest both retrospection and immediacy by a subtle combination of past and present tenses. It was a narrative technique that

opened new possibilities to later fiction writers, not only fellow Americans but also major innovators in South America who matured between 1950 and 1980.

Thus in the course of two generations, major artists in a single culture found alternate ways, based on colloquial resources, of restructuring the English language so as to transform an imported tongue into an unmistakably American one. When such different experiments occur it may be seen as a form of interior fertilization: the conventional has been opened up, so that modes can compete, merge, or conflict with suviving orthodox structures. It is a challenge to later generations of artists, journalists and educators to choose because Invention, in Williams' sense, has established new linguistic frontiers; Invention has made an old language new and contrived utterances distinctive to the new society.

Other new cultures have not developed comparably rich alternate modes of self-expression; they are usually characterized by only one major assault upon conventional syntax and vocabulary, the major innovative writer being followed by younger imitators: Maurice Duggan followed Frank Sargeson in New Zealand, and João Ribeiro followed João Guimarães Rosa in Brazil.

But perhaps more significant is the exterior fertilization that has been taking place with increasing frequency in recent years. This occurs when artists in one new culture learn from artists in another new culture. For more than a hundred years Walt Whitman's influence has been pervasive in many South American countries and Faulkner's saga of Yoknapatawpha County has influenced the making of fictional territories by South American novelists. Now the influence of Pablo Neruda, García Márquez and Jorge Luis Borges travels northwards and young writers in the United States and Canada gain techniques and sustenance from South Americans sources. Perhaps the emerging pattern is that new cultures now have the strength and maturity to nourish other new cultures.

(6)

Summary

In the making of new cultures the distinctive processes are bestowing names, re-shaping imported and indigenous values and fashioning a unique mode of self-articulation. These experiences contribute to modes of perception that have no counterpart in older societies. The new literatures dramatize these processes because, generally, artists in new cultures remain aware of the formative cultural forces; they know the arbitrariness of human values. It is easier for ruling elites in older societies to diminish Invention by appealing to tradition than to convince intelligent persons in new societies that an absolute scale of values dominates their cultural formation.

Restlessness is the mark of new cultures — whether in the pragmatic post-protestant societies of North America, Australia and New Zealand, in the explosive insular societies of the Caribbean, or in the violence-prone socially revolutionary societies of catholic South America. Process, not fixity, is the unavoidable inheritance and the great writers of new societies have analyzed this restlessness in their work; by doing so they have gained personal articulation but they have also contributed to the radical analysis of their cultural formation.

In making such explorations, new-world literary artists tend to centre upon and dramatize four main areas in their culture's evolution: the origins of the new society; actual or symbolic journeys that extended the knowledge or values of the dominant culture; new psycho-social mores that upset traditional family structure; and socio-political experiences that have shaped the consciousness of the new society.

This does not imply that all artists in all new societies are vitally concerned with analyses of cultural formation. Not all Mexican painters have the cultural interests of Orozco, Diego Rivera or

Siqueiros central to their vision; not all Canadian novelists re-create Canadian historical experiences in the manner of Rudy Wiebe or reveal Canadian responses to reality by inventing an imaginary county such as Margaret Laurence's Manawaka. But enough do show awareness, concern and analytical penetration so that patterns of commitment and response, representative of involvement with their culture's evolution, can be discerned. We shall now survey each of the four main areas of cultural evolution.

1. *Australian Letters*, Vol. 1. No. 3 (April 1958), pp.38-40.
2. Gutteridge, *A True History of Lambton County* (Ottawa, Oberon) p.27.
3. Williams, *Paterson* (New York, 1948) p.65.
4. Ringuet, *Trente arpents* (Montréal et Paris, 1966) p.13.
5. All translations in the book are my own and tend in most cases to differ from previously published versions.
6. White, *The Tree of Man* (London, 1956) p.3.
7. Sargeson, *Collected Stories 1935-1963* (Auckland, 1964), p.157.
8. Guimarães Rosa, *Grande Sertão: Veredas* (Rio de Janeiro, eighth edition), p.9.
9. Hemingway, *The Short Stories* (New York, 1938), p.209.
10. Faulkner, *The Unvanquished* (New York, 1965), p.3.

Chapter Two

ORIGINS: PERSONS AND PLACES

By naming them he made them.
"Cook's Mountains," P.K. Page

(1)

Although the origins of old cultures are obscured in the mists of preliteracy, the beginnings of new cultures can be exactly determined. The values carried by first explorers, settlers, missionaries and administrators, together with some of the basic values that structured the lives of the indigenous population, are recorded and can be referred to by later generations. In contrast to the origins of old societies there is an abundance of data. This allows new-world artists, if they wish, to review the records and examine the founding values of their society. As they seek, layer by layer to uncover the processes by which the current value-system has been formed, they have the advantage of being able to begin with recognizable intelligences arriving at particular places within a mathematically determined space and time — Christopher Columbus making landfall at Guanahaní on 12 October, 1492, or James Cook sighting the North Island of New Zealand at 2:00 p.m. on Saturday, 17 October, 1769.

Therefore an awareness of origins remains hauntingly persistent in new cultures. It is the society's first developmental pivot, the examination of which can serve to refresh an artist's primal vision, reconfirm his belief in the founding ideals, or justify his disgust at the corruptness in which the new society began and has continued. By evoking the culture's local beginnings a writer can dramatize attitudes for defining, renewing or replacing the founding values.

A new culture begins with the bestowal of new place names. The beginning of the new, therefore, is the act of naming; this function is usually associated with other symbolic actions representative of the name-bestower's value system, all of which reveal the newcomers' first confrontation with necessity in the unknown territory. Nowhere is the process more fascinating than in the accounts of Columbus' first landfall in 1492.

After sailing westwards for thirty-three days Columbus found landfall — the island of Guanahaní. He came ashore and made contact with the inhabitants, exchanging simple gifts. Over the next two weeks, with the help of some of these natives pressed into service aboard his caravels, Columbus sighted, charted and landed on other islands of the Bahamas before eventually arriving at the largest and most wondrous of the islands — Colba, or Cuba. Eagerly he gave names to his discoveries; but, of course, he was only renaming places that the local inhabitants had named long before. Columbus' Letter to the Sovereigns, addressed to his sponsors King Ferdinand and Queen Isabella of Spain, reveals both his understandable delight and his processes of thought as he voyaged from island to island.

á la primera que yo fallé puse nombre 'San Salvador', á comemoración de Su Alta Magestad, el qual maravillosamente todo esto ha dado; los Indios la llaman 'Guanahani'; á la segunda puse nombre 'la isla de Santa María de Concepción'; á la tercera 'Fernandina'; á la quarta 'la Ysabela'; á la quinta 'la isla Juana', é así á cada una nombre nuevo.[1]

On the first island I found I placed the name San Salvador, in commemoration of The Divine Majesty through whom all this has been wondrously achieved; the Indians call it Guanahaní; to the second island I gave the name 'the island of the Virgin of the Immaculate Conception'; to the third, Ferdinand; to the fourth, Isabella; to the fifth, Juan, and so to each I gave a new name.

Relief at being saved from peril is a sensation common to all travellers; but Columbus' choice of name for his first landfall represents far more than mere gratitude to a guiding deity. He is consciously laying on names in a ritual manner; like baptism the procedure was calculated to bring the unknown into christian hierarchical relationship. It was assumed that what lay outside orthodox relationship was inferior; what was brought in was rendered worthy. By his laying-on of names, therefore, Columbus established christian relationship with the unknown islands and imposed on them a christian and Spanish hierarchy of values.

The first name celebrated the male catholic deity; the second invoked celestial female power in the name of the Virgin of the Immaculate Conception — a figure of worship to which Columbus was addicted. Then, after establishing the spiritual hierarchy, he set up a hierarchy of material, or political, values by naming successive islands after the embodiments of God's power on earth — his sponsors Ferdinand and Isabella and their heir-apparent, Juan. So firm are the hierarchies of value in his mind that he acted in a mechanical fixated manner. Utterly insignificant islands received the names of God, the mother of God, the Spanish King and Queen. But the largest and most wondrously scenic of the islands was the fifth which received the name of Juan, the least important personage in the theological-political elite. Ironically history perpetuated none of Columbus' names and this island soon reverted to its original name — Cuba.[2]

It is interesting to see the ways in which some writers in the twentieth century draw upon the records of Columbus' arrival in the Caribbean to examine the origins of their culture.

(2)

The first of these is the great Cuban fiction writer Alejo Carpentier. In 1962 he published *El siglo de las luces*. Its historical

scope and textured prose make it one of the great narratives dramatizing Caribbean experience. In one magnificent sequence Carpentier evokes Columbus' arrival. He does this by contrasting the motivating myths of the natives — soon to be indiscriminately named
"indians" — with the motivating myths of the Europeans. The Ba-
hamian islanders had earlier migrated from the mainland impelled
by a faith that somewhere across the waters was a Promised Land;
there they would establish social supremacy and experience a new
life. Carpentier refers to them as the People of Totemic Power. They
poured forth across the islands, legitimizing their seizure by virtue
of their faith. But their attempts at settlement were disrupted by the
arrival of Europeans in ships so enormous they dwarfed the migrants' small canoes. Still the islanders made assaults upon the Spanish caravels; but as with any expanding empire, the power that con-
trols the superior technology prevails. Carpentier does not depict
the futility of the physical conflict; instead he focuses on the similar-
ity of the contestants' legitimizing myths. For Columbus also was
seeking a Promised Land and lived with the conviction that some
celestial agency would guide and reward him for exploratory efforts. In Carpentier's sonorous words:

> Dos tiempos históricos, inconciliables, se afrontaban en esa
> lucha sin tregua posible, que oponía el Hombre de los To-
> tems al Hombre de la Teología. Porque, súbitamente, el Ar-
> chipiélago en litigio se había venido vuelto un Archipiélago
> Teológico. Las islas mudaban de identidad integrándose en
> el Auto Sacramental del Gran Teatro del Mundo. La pri-
> mera isla conocida por un invasor venido de un continente
> inconcebible par el ente de acá, había recibido el nombre de
> Cristo, al quedar plantada una primera cruz, hecha de ra-
> mas, en su orilla. Con la segunda habíase remontado a la
> Madre, al llamarla Santa María de la Concepción. Las Antil-
> las se transformaban en un inmenso vitral, traspasado de
> luces donde los Donadores estaban ya presentes en el con-

torno de Fernandina y de la Isabella . . . Dando un salto de
milenos, pasaba este Mar Mediterráneo a hacerse heredero
del otro Mediterráneo, recibiendo, con el trigo y el latín, el
Vino y la Vulgata, la Imposición de los Signos Cristianos. [3]

Two historical periods that were irreconcilable confronted
one another in this struggle where no truce was possible.
The People of Totemic Power faced the People of Theological Power. Suddenly the Archipelago had changed into a
Theological Archipelago and become subject to dispute.
These islands were changing their identity, becoming integrated into an *auto sacramental* in the Great Theatre of the
World. The first island that had been discovered by an invader from a continent inconceivable to the natives had received the name of Christ; and there was left planted on its
shores the first cross made of branches. For the second island the invader had regressed to the name of Mother, and
called it the Virgin of the Immaculate Conception. The An-
tilles were being transformed into an immense stained-glass
window, flooded by sunlight, where the sponsors, Ferdinand and Isabella, were soon to be present . . . With a leap
of some thousands of years this Mediterranean Sea had become heir to the other Mediterranean, receiving bread and
latin, wine and the vulgate, the laying-on of christian
symbols.

Carpentier's prose is rich in implications, some of which are
not transferable out of Spanish cultural tradition. He suggests the
coming of latin christianity to the Americas by renaming the Caribbean Archipelago — baptizing it so that it becomes a second Mediterranean Sea, one of the earliest homes of European christianity.
The superb metaphor of a stained-glass window, such as one might
see in a European cathedral, refers to major technological achievements in mediæval Europe; but at the same time it infers the sure

conquest that certitude in technology combined with dogmatic faith can destructively produce.

Columbus' account stresses the amiability of the natives and the ease of contact between them and the newcomers. Carpentier, on the other hand, sees the very first meeting of the two groups as one of irreconcilable conflict. In his view, when the People of Totemic Power meet the People of Theological Power, there can be no truce. The encounter and the laying-on of names anticipated future centuries of repression by institutionalized religion, civil law and military might.

Carpentier's ironic statement is that the new world, from its very beginning as a European dependency, was being incorporated into an *auto sacramental* — a vivid public drama performed with liturgical deliberation throughout Spain on holidays with the object of reinforcing the spectators' orthodox belief. The *auto sacramental* was unexamined dogma disguised as mass entertainment. Carpentier's implication is that the values of his Caribbean world, which he inherited four hundred years after Columbus' arrival, were to a large extent predetermined: the initial bestowing of names and the accompanying ritual, converted the whole area from one value-system to another. The action was irreversible and certain consequences unchangeable. Any freedom to choose values for constructing their own culture was non-existent for the peoples of the Spanish new world.

A similar perspective and judgement have been offered by other artists of the Caribbean and South America. In *El otōno del patriarcha* (1976), the Columbian writer Gabriel García Márquez focuses his irony upon the political consequences of predetermined totalistic values. The novel exposes the consciousness of a brutal dictator in the first decades of the twentieth century whose country borders the Caribbean; in examining the aged patriarch's paranoia, García Márquez uncovers the layers of experience that have contributed to the making of South American cultures. At one point in the novel he looks back to the new world's origins.

He shows the half-crazed, half-mythic patriarchal figure, who still wields absolute power, overlooking the Caribbean; the dictator recalls a distant October day when everyone in his presidential palace suddenly appeared wearing red caps. An air of festivity prevailed. In response to his enquiry he was told strangers had arrived; they seemed extraordinarily excited at meeting the inhabitants and, in an effort to calm them down, the natives engaged in a simple joyous exchange of gifts:

> y nos cambiaban todo lo que teníamos por estos bonetes colorados y estas sartas de pepitas de vidrio que nos colgábamos en el pescuezo por hacerles gracia [4]

> and they exchanged everything that we were offering for these coloured caps and these glass beads that we hung round our necks so as to please them

Phrases such as *bonetes colorados* and *sartas de pepitas de vidrio* echo Columbus' own narrative detailing his encounter with the islanders of Guanahaní. But García Márquez' recounting of the event allows little of Columbus' joyous simplicity in the achievement to remain. He reminds us that innocent first trading prepared the way for the most colossal, centuries-long exploitation; through the years countless persons have been cruelly dispossessed by the many traders and administrators who followed Columbus. Operating clandestinely, the ruling elite installed as figureheads power-crazed dictators like the aged patriarch so that the ravishment of people and land could continue unabated.

As the dictator continues looking from the presidential palace his muddled gaze sees — or imagines — the same three caravels in which Columbus sailed to the new world in the late fifteenth century; and lying close to shore is a rusting battleship left behind by United States marines when they put him in power early in the twentieth century. The president's mind, bereft by paranoia and age of divisions into chronological time, transmutes all events into a timeless, or mythic, present. García Márquez' implication is that, whatever the historical time, his culture is always characterized by a willingness to barter basic values for trinkets from invaders. Columbus' beads were followed four hundred years later by United States battleships. In García Márquez' vision, the beginning was itself a degradation; and different forms of degradation have followed, permeating the culture throughout its development.

A similar distress at degradation arising from the dominance of alien imposed values runs through Edward Brathwaite's presentation of Caribbean origins in *The Arrivants: A New World Trilogy* (1973). The Barbadian poet is outraged by the contemporary sense of unbelonging and racial hostility experienced by many black West Indians in the twentieth century. They often encounter the full force of prejudice when they leave their native islands seeking work in the United States or Europe. Brathwaite contrasts these modern migrants setting out with dreams that are both hopeful and naive with the dreams of the first Spanish migrants to the new world. He imagines Columbus endowed with comparable expectant wonderment as his caravels drifted towards the Bahamas. Not even squawking birds could upset the man's equanimity; he is shown continuing to meditate with deep composure on his belief that the promised land will appear.

Brathwaite's presentday narrator, writing with the historical hindsight that for five centuries the Caribbean people have been murdered, enslaved or impoverished, wonders if Columbus privately entertained a vision of the mass suffering that would follow his arrival; certainly Columbus delighted in and described the natural beauties of the islands; but he also informed the King of Spain that subjugation of the natives could be easily accomplished. Did Columbus ever dream, in his fixed resolute mind, of the shattered bones and whiplash discipline that would transform the islands' peace?

Brathwaite's exploration of origins leaves the question hovering as if the lack of a clear answer would stimulate the contemporary people of the new world to enquire further in an effort at clearer self-definition.

Far harsher in its rhetoric and more forthright in its rejection of the great discoverer Columbus is Pablo Neruda's *Canto general* (1950). Like Brathwaite, the Chilean poet identifies with the centuries-long oppression of the people who share his culture. To stress the disruptive effects caused by the first Europeans, Neruda presents a lyrical, idyllic portrait of the new world before their coming.

> Los monos tranzaban un hilo
> interminablemente erótico
> en las riberas de la aurora
> derribando muros de polen [5]

> The monkeys wove a thread
> that was endlessly erotic
> on the shores of the dawn
> overturning walls of pollen

The land, in its geophysical naturalness, is alive, fecund, proudly unique. It contains the promise of continual creation and self-renewal.

Then the Europeans came to Guanahaní — "los carniceros desolaton las islas" (The butchers laid waste the islands). [6] Atrocities were commonplace, genocide a mode of subjugation. In Neruda's phrase, the virgin of the garrote replaced the virgin of the immaculate conception.

> Sólo quedaban huesos
> rígidamente colocados
> en forma de cruz, para mayor
> gloria de Dios y de los hombres [7]

There remained just bones
rigidly stuck together
in the shape of a cross, for the greater
glory of God and the benefit of some men.

Neruda's bitterness, achieved by savage juxtapositions of imagery and the wrenching of word-meanings from their usual associations, appears limitless as he evokes his culture and the South American historical experience. He does not even mention Columbus by name as he presents the European arrival in the new world; Neruda's implication is that Columbus was historically negligible compared to the mass butchery and exploitation that followed his coming.

In these evocations of cultural origins, disruption is the characterizing element. The discovery of the territories was a disruption in itself; but it was only a modest herald to the cruelty, repression and centuries-long exploitation that followed. A great deal of later history was predetermined by the absolutist values, often supported by absolutist theology, that structured the mentality of the early commercialists, administrators, missionaries and adventurers. The deduction is that the evolving cultures, to the present-day, have never recovered from their disastrous beginnings. Artists' analyses of cultural origins in the Caribbean and South America tend to be bleakly depressing.

(3)

It is like passing from darkness to light to move from Caribbean origins to South Pacific origins, from fifteenth-century absolutist theology to eighteenth-century empirical values. Instead of disruption, a sense of integration characterizes cultural origins and evolution.

In the eighteenth-century England was the home of empiricism. Precise measurement and demonstrable data were replacing

grandiose assertions about the nature of God and cosmos as legitimate knowledge. The scientific desideratum was a world known
with ever more detailed exactitude. In this regard Captain James
Cook was a product of his age and a model of professional responsibility. His navigational skill accompanied his precision in patiently
recording minute details of geophysical phenomena. Although
authoritarian, he took pains to establish humane shipboard conditions between officers and men and, unlike many of his fellow cap-
tains, was able to maintain the respect of subordinates.

One of the finest evocations of the man and his achievements is Kenneth Slessor's poem "Five Visions of Captain Cook".
While still a schoolboy in Australia, Slessor had been fascinated by
the navigational feats that had led to the founding of his native land;
in later years, he studied old seafarers' accounts of travelling to the
South Seas, learned more about Cook and gathered a sense of the
awe and mystery which surrounded both place and person.

For although his acts seemed eminently rational, Cook was
sometimes impelled by motivations that were not at all rational. One
of these resulted in his first landfall in Australia. When prevailing
South Pacific winds became intense and threatened his ships' safety,
Cook could have followed the prudent and logical example of earlier voyagers like Bougainville and sailed northwards to safer waters;
instead he made the extraordinary decision to turn west and sail
into the perils of a lee shore. In that direction lay Australia. In Slessor's words:

> So Cook made choice, so Cook sailed westabout
> So men write poems in Australia. [8]

Slessor's five "visions" of Cook offer different perspectives on the
man and his achivement. Through the eyes of a twentieth-century
sailor, eighteenth-century officers and midshipmen, and one aged
memory-haunted mariner who had sailed with him, Cook the man
is presented. Slessor emphasizes that all see the magic and mystery

that lay like some impenetrable reality behind the man's disciplined
rational behaviour. The wondrousness of the places visited adds to
the five narrators' general sense of indefinable awe:

> Not all the botany
> Of Joseph Banks, hung pensive in a porthole,
> Could find the Latin for this loveliness.

Although both Cook and Banks, his scientific associate,
represent the unique human power to name and hence transfer
cultural values, the astonishing beauty of shoreline and reef were
always larger than the human capacity to enclose the natural phenomena in words; the "suck-mouth tides", "half moons of surf" and
"flying blood of cardinal birds" retain an awesomeness that exceeds
the human power to name. Slessor's poem, while evoking the origins of Australian culture, also magnificently dramatizes the fragil-
ity of human effort when contrasted with the immeasurable mystery
enfolding all life.

In Cook's own writing, the poet is hidden. His prose is blunt
but craftsmanlike, showing methodical organization and precise
recording of observed data. In his account of the First Voyage he
records a dispute among the officers; the question was whether
Moreton Bay on the Queensland coast was, or was not, the source of
a river. Contrary winds prevented Cook from approaching nearer
land and determining the issue. So he summarizes the cases for and
against the possibility of a river-mouth and then adds:

> but should any one be desirous of doing it that may come
> after me this place may always be found by three hills which
> lay to the northward of it in the Latitude of 26°53's. These
> hills lay but a little way inland and not far from each other,
> they are very remarkable on account of their singular form
> of elevation which very much resembles glass houses which
> occasioned my giving them that name, the northernmost of

the three is the highest and largest. There are likewise several other peaked hills inland to the northward of these but
they are not near so remarkable.[9]

After stating the problem and providing exact data to enable later
comers to investigate and resolve the issue, Cook ascribes a name to
the encompassing hills that will help others to identify the location.
His name is based on a simple analogy, a private recollection from
his British homeland. He is careful to supply a reason for his arbitrary nomenclature, as though a poetic image or analogy had to be
justified.

Yet two hundred years later the place and the name he had
bestowed on it, which has survived into the twentieth-century, int-
rigued the visiting Anglophone Canadian poet P.K. Page. In a short
poem, "Cook's Mountains", she describes how travelling by car in an
unfamiliar country she — or an imaginary narrator — saw the
strangely-formed mountains rise out of the rain-forest; the car driv-
er informed her that these were the Glass-House Mountains. Suddenly the narrator becomes more conscious of the origin of the new
culture she is experiencing; it is not her own culture, but she comes
from one which shares the same language, social predispositions,
rain-forest, mountains and — not least — the achievements of
James Cook. She states with firm exactitude:

> By naming them he made them.
> They were there
> before he came
> but they were not the same.
> It was his gaze
> that glazed each one.[10]

Although the mountains existed before Cook's explorations, since
his coming and naming a later visitor can see them only through his
naming-process. His analogy of their glimmering shapes with Eng-

lish glass-houses, seemingly a random association less important to him than the record of precise data, emerge in P.K. Page's telling phrase from "the dark's imagination":

> Like mounds of mica,
> hive-shaped hothouses,
> mountains of mirror glimmering
> they form
> in diamond panes behind the tree ferns of
> the dark's imagination,
> burn and shake
> the lovely light of Queensland like a bell
> reflecting Cook upon a deck
> his tongue
> silvered with paradox and metaphor.

Page, like Slessor, marvels at the mystery behind Cook's rational intelligence, at the poet behind the professional navigator, at the power of paradox and metaphor behind the recording of factual data. In effect, the mountains blend two strangenesses — their own unique shapes rising above the rain-forest and Cook's poetic analogy. The two can never be separated; instead, they represent the culture's healthy evolution and sturdy accretion of values.

There is a direct, practical quality in much of Cook's name-bestowing. The same characteristic was to appear later in the eighteenth-century during the explorations of the North Pacific by George Vancouver, who had served an apprenticeship with Cook. Names of British government officials, Admiralty administrators and ships officers remain to demarcate places along the Pacific North West coast. Eighteenth-century protestant empiricism preferred a national hierarchy of power and homely everyday practicalities as sources of names to a grandiose gathering of protective deities and mythological saints that were ever ready to catholic consciousness.

This type of name bestowing and the belief in accretive values that accompnaies it is finely dramatized in some of the fiction of Howard O'Hagan. A man belonging to the Western Canadian wilderness by birth and youthful experience, O'Hagan understood the need to clothe with words the bare reality of a new land. Descriptive language gave voice to a mute landscape; and once the voice had spoken, it could never be silenced or forgotten. This is richly exemplified in a short story called "The White Horse".[11]

The scene is the foothills of the Canadian Rockies. By the 1930s some places had not yet received names. "In the valley only the creek was named and one mountain, called Black Mountain. All the hills were nameless." Nick has pioneered there for more than thirty years and prefers places that bear names to those that do not. "It was more home-like and warmer to have names about." As a young man, he had been a packer in the foothills, delivering stores to survey camps, one of which had been run by a Mr. Bedford. He was an English surveyor who, despite the pain suffered from the cold climate, remained extremely fastidious about hygiene and dress. All this formality impressed Nick the backwoodsman so that when a colt was born to his mare, Nick respectfully named him after Mr. Bedford; he broke in the colt as a pack horse and noticed that like his English namesake the animal always tended to keep a social distance between himself and others.

But over the years man and horse grow old together. Thirty years after completing both survey and rail line, Bedford is the only horse remaining from the early pioneering days. He is the only "abiding link" with local history and Nick's youth.

Then, in the 1930s, during a winter of heavy snow, Bedford is trapped in a growth of jack-pine and freezes to death. Nick discovers the body and then returns to his isolated cabin to engage in a paradoxical act. He writes out a notice stating the horse has been lost and offers a reward for finding the animal. He puts the notice where passersby would see it. Nick knew they would not spend their time looking for Bedford; that was not the intent of his notice. Instead, his scattered neighbours would know "that he was a good horse. If he had not been a good horse, his owner would not have offered a reward. Those men who were neighbours would understand. They would not go to look for the white horse."

At winter's end, one of Nick's neighbours sets up a wooden marker on the trail out of town. He was an immigrant who wanted all the places of his new country to carry names as did all the places of his native Norway: on the marker he had carved the name "Bedford Pass."

> Hunting parties and tourists would see it. People would ask how the pass got its name. Someone would tell them about Bedford, the white horse, the last horse left in the valley from the early days.

So British attitudes and technology, surveying, railway construction, packing supplies, immigration from Europe, hunting, touring — the whole human history of the area's development and the massive achievement of domesticating a wilderness would be enclosed in the name.

> Bedford was now a name. The wolves would not have him. He would outlast flesh and bone and hide and hair. He would endure so long as men climbed rivers to their source and spoke into the wind the pass's name they travelled.

This type of naming suggests an accretion of positive values through the spread of human effort through several generations. In appraising origins, the recognition is that the geophysical environment has been changed by personal valour and the imaginative application of intelligence: Cook deciding to sail westwards to a lee shore, the appreciation of the narrator, in P.K. Page's poem, of the name given the Glass-House Mountains, or Nick and the Norwegian immigrant combining obliquely as neighbours in a wilderness to name a pass in memory of a horse and an era. Unlike name bestowals drawn from alien church calendars and ecclesiastical mythologies, this process recognizes the material transformation of reality. Necessity has been confronted by human contrivance: where mystery and reason combine to produce intelligent naming and a retrospective appraisal sees in the process a basis for humane values, the culture shows a healthful evolutionary integration. This judgement and perspective are far removed from the anguish of disruption, exploitation and predetermination that, in the judgement and perspective of some writers, characterize the cultural origins of Caribbean and South American societies.

(4)

There is a further judgement on cultural origins and development in which acute disillusionment is precariously balanced against a passionate will to renewal. It is most clearly evident in the work of many major poets and fiction writers from Francophone Canada during the years from 1950 to 1980.

Quebec's founding values were French, Catholic and absolutist. They shaped a relatively harmonious society based on social and spiritual submissiveness. Within narrow and rigid bounds, the society produced the skills to confront a harsh geophysical necessity and survive.

Then, after the British conquest of Quebec, came the territory's secession from France. Although the colonial ties had never been as strong as was desirable for sturdy economic growth, the shock of separation for the Quebecois was traumatic and extended over several centuries. Turning inward to preserve its distinctiveness against the alternate values offered by United States' and Anglophone Canadian models, Quebec culture survived by perpetuating past values. Under the guidance of spiritual and political leaders, traditional integrity was preserved; but the price was a static society in which submission to authority was a virtue. At a time when the dominant Anglophone cultures developed empirical modes of scientific enquiry and social control, Quebec reverted to mediæval belief in the ideal of unchangingness. Inevitably there had to come a time of reckoning — a period when self-scrutiny of basic values had to be undertaken.

This occurred primarily between 1950 and 1980, when young poets and novelists delved into examining the origins and growth of Quebec culture and, like their South American counterparts, concluded that indigenous cultural development had always been distorted. The native land had never been free; it had always been a victim of predetermined values. But now alternates were available; a time to choose was at hand; it was possible to alter current conditions; unchangingness must change.

Young poets protesting social, intellectual and technological stagnation both recognized and tried to abolish the founding, traditional values. These were seen as belonging to a period of pre-history that had shaped a false consciousness. In order to grow, they must be rejected. Then a new consciousness would appear to augur the new age when the Quebecois would take full possession of environment and history.

The poet's function, therefore, was to name new origins that would become part of the new consciousness. The metaphor used was a voyage of discovery. In the words of Yves Préfontaine: "L'homme québécois en est aux premiers balbutiements de sa propre découverte de l'Amérique."[12] ("Quebecois are at the stage of making the first stammering utterances about their own discovery of America.") The poet gives direction to these stammering discoveries by helping to name anew the vast space which is Quebec; thus he can contribute to transforming "its chilly silence, its snowy nothingness."[13]

His first function is to dramatize the contemporary cultural condition. A static frozen landscape, locked in wintry isolation, is the metaphor used by many writers to suggest the encompassing reality of the stifled culture. Préfontaine's "Peuple inhabité" is a major poem about the dilemma of a poet belonging to a culture awaiting new roots:

> J'habite un espace où le froid triomphe de l'herbe, où la grisaille règne en lourdeur sur des fantômes d'arbres.

> J'habite en silence un peuple qui sommeille, frileux sous le givre de ses mots. J'habite un peuple dont se tarit la parole frêle et brusque.[14]

> I live in a vast space where white cold triumphs over green grass, where greyness lowers its weight over phantom trees.

> I live in silence among a people who sleep shivering under the frost of their words. I live in a people whose acute but fragile language is slowly drying up.

Humanly established geographical borders disappear — the narrator lives in a "space" not a "country"; a primal silence enfolds everyone sharing the space but it is a non-creative, or infertile, silence. There is the ominous fear that the language belonging to the area is in danger of disappearing.

> Une neige de fatigue étrangle avec donceur le pays que j'habite . . .

> J'habite un peuple qui ne s'habite plus.

> A snow of tiredness softly strangles the place where I live . . .

> I live in a people who no longer live.

Despite the desperation that arises from such depths of cultural sterility, the narrator still cries aloud against the condition of things. Perhaps the populace will awaken. And there is still some life-force in the land that invades his blood, quickens his desire and provokes him to rage against current conditions with "a poverty of words that shine brightly and then disappear."

The vision is of a people who suffer, even though they are themselves mostly unaware of their cultural deprivation. The poet's alienation is also from his own people: he knows the poverty of their deprivation, they do not. His dual alienation — from impoverished populace and stifled culture — serves to sharpen in him the urge to kindle new beginnings.

One of the great poems expressing personal anguish and the desire to transform the condition of things is Gaston Miron's "Héritage de la tristesse". The image presented of the land suggests its prehistoric barrenness. Unlike Neruda's images of exuberant fertility in his imagining of the South American continent before Columbus' arrival, Miron's Quebec is a beautiful but sterile place. The rich orchestrated language contrasts with the description of cultural bareness:

> Il est triste et pêle-mêle dans les étoiles tombées
> livide, muet, nulle part et effaré, vaste fantôme
> il est ce pays seul avec lui-même et neiges et rocs
> un pays que jamais ne rejoint le soleil natal[15]

> It is sad and confused amid the fallen stars
> pale, dumb, nowhere, fearful, an enormous phantom
> — thus is the land, alone with its own being, with snow and rocks
> a land that is never more connected to its life-giving sun

Islolation is seen as a negative force, producing silence; it frustrates the will to connect with other beings, to love, to gain self-fulfilment ("un desir d'être"). Passively the land — and by implication the culture — waits, despoiled and having minimal hope.

But winds are the unpredictable forces of the cosmos. Miron evokes their inescapable, if uncontrollable, power to suggest the change that should come over "the face of a lost people":

> vents telluriques, vents de l'âme, vents universels
> vents ameutez-nous, et de vos bras de fleuve ensemble
> enserrez son visage de peuple abîmé, redonnez-lui
> la chaleur

> winds of the earth, of the spirit, of the universe
> winds come clashing together among us, and with your
> arms of river
> embrace the face of a lost people, give them back
> a living warmth

The controlled rhetoric contrasts with the uncontrolled energies, or spirits, being evoked. These climactic commands form a magnificent cry to arouse people so that they may enter their full humanity — a fulfilment always denied those who suffer from any type of cultural deprivation.

The images of wintry desolation and sterile statue-like people appear in the work of other Quebec poets of Miron's generation and acquaintance. Roland Giguère, Paul-Marie Lapointe, Michèle Lalonde, Yves Préfontaine, Paul Chamberland all show a depth of despair which emanates from a sense that one's heritage is sterile and its values grown false. To abolish the past as an intellectual act is a gesture of love; from the destruction, even though it involves a degree of self-annihilation, it is believed creativity will come. Because the criticism of the culture goes to its fundamentals, the basis for renewal must also reach to fundamentals. It must, to use the metaphors of the poets, penetrate through the frozen soil and the plundered veins of earth, through the sterile popular consciousness to the origins of place and people. The exploratory effort, it is hoped, will preserve the threatened language; for, above all, it is language that must reinvigorate the culture and the consciousness. And this use of language requires the establishment of new names — positive, hope-filled, fertile, amorous names.

Roland Giguère expresses the faith in cultural renewal in a fine poem "Paysage dépaysé". In common with fellow poets, he evokes the sensation of loss and alienation with the familiar images of desolate snowy landscape. A storm has been raging for a long time, lacerating the people, crowning them with thorns, reducing them to mere cries in the night. From the agony, culture and consciousness grew — in separation, not in harmony; and the alienation remains into the present. Giguère concludes his poem with a series of modulated negations which subtly become transformed into a final quiet assertion.

> le paysage n'était plus le même
> la paysage était sombre
> le paysage ne nous allait plus comme un gant
> n'avait plus les couleurs de notre jeunesse
> le paysage le beau paysage n'était plus beau
> il n'y avait plus de ruisseaux
> plus de fougères plus d'eau
> il n'y avait plus rien
>
> le paysage était à refaire.[16]

> the landscape was no longer the same
> the landscape was dark
> the landscape no longer fitted us like a glove
> it no longer had the colours of our youth
> the landscape the beautiful landscape was no
>   longer beautiful
> there were no more streams
> no more ferns no more water
> there was no longer anything
>
> the landscape had to be made again.

The erosion of fertility is absolute so that a condition of nothingness finally prevails. Yet Giguère's negative lyricism finally leads to a positive recommendation.

More positive and more lyrical is Gatien Lapoint's "Ton Pays". The poem is a delicate encouragement for persons to look through the snow, the sterility, and the vast pain of the populace; to accept the human reality of reaching out to amend current conditions; and, in so doing, to see into the centre of things. The glimpse thus gained is not into some despair-filled heart of darkness but rather into the mystery of potential — of naming anew and thus bringing to birth new human values.

> Si tu ouvres les yeux,
> Si tu poses les mains
> Sur la neige, les oiseaux, les arbres, les bêtes
> Patiemment, doucement,
> Avec tout le poids de ton coeur . . .
>
> Si tu embrasses chaque mort de ton enfance
> Patiemment, doucement,
> Avec tout le poids de ton desespoir:
>
> Alors ton pays pourra naître.[17]

> If you open your eyes,
> If you put your hands
> On the snow, the birds, the trees, the beasts
> Patiently, softly,
> With all the weight of your heart . . .
>
> If you embrace each death of your childhood
> Patiently, softly,
> With all the weight of your despair
>
> Then your country will be born.

Distress stemming from dissatisfaction with one's culture and its origins is alleviated by a passionate will to change conditions. The future offers new values. The future begins by taking time by the hand, abolishing the ignominious period of pre-history, and bestowing names. Gatien Lapointe's perspective, like that of his fellow anguished Quebec poets, belongs distinctively to a new-world environment.

(5)

Summary

To name is to take possession. Naming attempts to make the unfamiliar a part of the namer's familiar and preferred value-system. The poetry of naming, whether theological or empirical in its source, becomes part of the culture's origins. Artists of later generations can turn to this first developmental pivot in a culture, uncovering the original values in order to define, renew or replace them. When the new culture has achieved consistent growth, the founding experiences may be seen as healthily integrative and are evoked with sympathy and optimism. When the new culture appears corrupt, inert or subject to alien manipulations, the founding experiences are presented negatively. Disillusionment in an acute form tries to consign the whole experience to a period of pre-history, sometimes accompanying the rejection with a compensatory dream of a new beginning. This may derive, in part, from a new naming. What remains the same in these different new-world analyses is the common necessity to scrutinize origins, and from the scrutiny to seek understanding of cultural formation.

This necessity is finely conveyed by the Anglophone Canadian poet John Newlove in his poem "The Pride". It is essential to seek, he asserts,

> the knowledge of
> our origins, and where
> we are in truth,

whose land this is
and is to be.[18]

Newlove assumes, in common with many other writers from new cultures, that a definition of personal and collective consciousness in the present can be assisted by first understanding cultural origins. The hope is that this "journey to the seed", to use Alejo Carpentier's phrase, should both deepen self-assurance and illuminate future cultural developments.

Pablo Neruda uses an intensely physical metaphor to convey the same necessity for scrutinizing origins:

hundí la mano turbulenta y dulce
en lo más genital de lo terrestre[19]

I plunged my potent and tender hand
into the most procreative part of my native soil

Neruda urges a mental-sexual engagement with the land where forebears lived, worked and died; his belief, similar to Newlove's, is that a deeper knowledge of personal and collective consciousness will result. Each shares a distinctive new-world perspective. Each by radical analysis of his culture's evolution contributes to its further formation.

1. Jane, *Select Documents Illustrating the Four Voyages of Columbus*, (London, 1930), Vol. 1, pp. 2-3.
2. The modern names are Watling's Island, Rum Cay, Long Island, Crooked Island.
   See Morison, *Admiral of the Ocean Sea* (Boston, 1942).
3. Carpentier, *El siglo de las luces* (Mexico, 1965), p. 209.
4. García Márquez, *El otoño del patriarca* (Barcelona, 1975), p. 45.
5. Neruda, *Obras completas* (Buenos Aires, seg. ed. 1962), p. 300.
6. Neruda, p. 325.

7. Neruda, p. 325.

8. Slessor, *One Hundred Poems, 1919-1938* (Sydney, 1948), pp. 64-71.

9. Beaglehole (ed.) *The Voyage of the Endeavour 1768-1771* (Cambridge, 1955), p. 319.

10. Page, *Poems Selected and New* (Toronto, 1974), pp. 113-114.

11. O'Hagan, *The Woman Who Got on at Jasper Station and other Stories* (Denver, 1963), pp. 96-104.

12. Préfontaine, *Pays sans parole* (Ottawa, 1967), p. 7.

13. Préfontaine, p. 9.

14. Préfontaine, pp. 40-41.

15. Miron, *L'homme rapaillé* (Montreal, 1970), p. 49.

16. Giguère, *L'age de la parole* (Ottawa, 1965), p. 111.

17. *L'Action*, Vol. 59, Dec. 30, 1966, p. 9.

18. Newlove, *Black Night Window* (Toronto, 1968), pp. 105-111.

19. Neruda, p. 312.

Chapter Three:

PROCESSES: JOURNEYS

*The New World originated in hypocrisy and
genocide, so it is not a question, for us, of returning to an Eden or of creating Utopia.*
Derek Walcott

(1)

Fascination with origins — the root beginnings of a culture
— leads some new-world artists to concern themselves about the
later processes that have contributed to cultural formation. These
later processes in new societies usually depend on making journeys
— external journeys across seas to promote commercial ventures or
internal journeys within the country. Exploring, settling, exploiting
natural resources, establishing refuges for political or religious disi-
dents, and discovering the values held by native peoples are some
historical motivations for making journeys that directly or indirectly
have served to consolidate and extend the dominant culture within
a particular territory.

The artist's re-creation of journeys is often made as a radical
analysis of the culture's evolution. It attempts to find or define values that remain outside the experience of the dominant system. The
critical new-world artist, with Romantic self-assertiveness, seeks a
place away from immediate convention, where he may find alternative perspectives and new modes of measuring contemporary reality; he may often wish to avoid or escape from the predetermination
of values and perspective that any culture imposes on its partici-
pants. Hence his dramatization of journeys is frequently an expression of alternative values that oppose or challenge existing ones. His
narrative may begin by showing a cultural divisiveness; his protagonist enters on a journey that deepens his understanding of both the

culture and his own relationship to it; the narrative concludes by implying or indicating a potential for healing cultural wounds.

We shall look at four major novels from different new-world societies in which journeying is used as a narrative structure; the device enables authors to reveal their criticisms of society, expose part of the cultural formation and suggest the possibility for restoring perspectives blocked by current values.

(2)

Patrick White's vision of Australian development tends to be bleakly pessimistic, although relieved at times by satiric humour. As a young man he remained for many years divided in commitment between Australia, where he had spent his earliest years, and Europe where he had received much of his education; when he returned to Australia in his late thirties his criticisms of the culture were uniquely austere. He was harsh towards the many forms of cheerful extroversion and suburbanite consumerism; he saw the meretricious accepted by the democratic mass as having true worth; he agonized over the partial perceptions that so many people imagined were ennobling visions. To understand the complacency that underlay and encouraged such attitudes White set about exposing, in successive narratives, the experiences that contributed to this cultural formation.

One of his greatest successes is the novel *Voss* (1957). It is constructed around two journeys — one private and interior, the other exterior and historical. There is also the implication of a third anterior journey that had been made by the men and women who, in the first decades of the nineteenth century, established Sydney and New South Wales as a centre for commerce and mannered social intercourse.

The latter become subjects for White's humorous irony. The class of prosperous merchants and landowners who had settled the area had imported the lifestyle of the English country gentry; by the 1830s they had become sedulous imitators of attitudes and manners carried from the British homeland. In White's view a social routine of visits and balls occupied and vitiated the energies of the women; merchandizing, landowning and sheepfarming preoccupied the men. An atmosphere of leisurely security appeared to enfold all; but in the 1830s New South Wales was still a penal colony where the majority of servants and workers upon whom the ruling elite depended were convicted felons.

This fact does little to limit the self-satisfaction of the elite which had already eaten itself into "a stupor of mutton".[1] It insistently congratulates itself on the prosperity and progress of the colony: "Look at our homes and public edifices. Look at the devotion of our administrators, and the solid achievement of those men who are settling the land" (p. 25). White criticizes not the achievement but the self-complacency he sees as forming part of the new culture. A desire to imitate has produced a constrictive conformity. The new society is already characterized by limited perceptiveness and false standards for measuring persons and behaviour.

Standing more and more apart from the ruling elite's self-satisfaction is Laura Trevelyan. She shows at first a modest independence; she refuses, for instance, to accompany her family to the customary Sunday morning church service. Although this is only a first uncertain rejection of conventional practice, other rejections are to follow as she undertakes an interior journey to examine the values structuring contemporary behaviour; the deeper she travels, the more she understands how narrowing predetermined perceptions block personal vision. But the price for insight into any structuring values — social, economic, political or religious — is always aloneness. At the end of her interior journey Laura has the strength to choose a life of relative seclusion and turns her negative isolation into a positive resource: she finds major self-expression in teaching a later generation some parts of the intuitive insights she has gained.

Young Laura's inducement to undertake this frightening journey into intuitive understanding has been her brief meeting with Johann Ulrich Voss. He is an arrogant, self-obsessed German who has come to the colony to make an exploratory journey into the interior. He dreams of bestowing his name on some part of the country; apart from this, he is a relatively young, healthy and ambitious person, complete in himself. Although he and Laura meet on only a few occasions before he departs for the outback, they achieve a rare, part-mystical communication which survives their physical separation. Each experiences "the silence of solitary travel through infinity" (p. 120); they converse across the silence, solitude and space; and each becomes aware of the other's suffering, spiritual development. Finally, as their two journeys near completion, Laura in an ecstasy of fever, understands that Voss has died somewhere in the outback. She knows his mission has failed but her developed intuitive understanding reveals to her that in death and failure Voss is triumphant.

For, like her, journeying has transformed the person. His early arrogance was so vast he conceived God and cosmos within the purlieus of his egotism; a monstrous will-to-power had driven him onwards. But the immediate perils of outback travel and his uncertain relationships with other men forced upon him an appreciation of humility. His growing physical exhaustion parallelled the erosion of his Romantic conceit. Compelled by the dangers of his expedition to confront unconditional necessity, Voss learns that he can never possess the land by naming it or preparing it for other men's settlement; instead, a more powerful reality finally possesses him. Voss' real journey is from the arrogance of a self-conceived Romantic totality to the humility of being possessed by an external force. He learns: "The mystery of life is not solved by success, which is an end in itself, but in failure, in perpetual struggle, in becoming" (p. 267). White uses the incidents of Voss' journey to reveal his deepening consciousness of "becoming".

And Laura's inner journey — she does not leave constrictive Sydney society — bears a similar significance. Growing to realize the sterility of her mannered society's attitudes, she identifies with the pregnancy, labour and birth-pains of an emancipist servant; when the young woman dies, Laura feels deeper kinship with the Australian land as a consequence of the suffering she shared with the servant. She states on one occasion: "A country does not develop through the prosperity of a few landowners and merchants, but out of the sufferings of the humble" (p. 234). Laura's spiritual journey ends when mannered society, always triumphant, is intent on enshrining the dead Voss' exploratory accomplishments in history books and statues. She has the inner clarification to assert in the face of such facile institutionalizing: "Knowledge was never a matter of geography. Quite the reverse, it overflows all maps that exist. Perhaps true knowledge only comes of death by torture in the country of the mind" (p. 440).

In writing *Voss* White chose to dramatize a period of conflicting values in Australian history. He used the 1830s, a crucial time in Australian development, to pose a fundamental question: what is the "true knowledge" upon which cultural and personal foundations may be built? Imitativeness of English social values was an inadequate base for any lasting structure; commercial expansionism was in itself insufficient; and a Faustian intellectual rapacity, symbolized in part by the immigrant explorer's early journeying, also had its perils and futilities. The only base, White concludes, for a viable culture and personal fulfillment must emerge from the knowledge formed by private and prolonged confrontations with necessity. Laura's journey and Voss' final awareness dramatize this confrontation and show the solitary anguish suffered by those who seek alternative perspectives to measure self and society.

(3)

The Diviners (1974) by the Anglophone Canadian fiction writer Margaret Laurence, dramatizes through narrative, symbolic characters and major journeys the joining of distinct powerful strands in Canada's cultural formation. Six journeys structure the narrative. They range from journeys made by first settlers in the unexplored regions of Manitoba and Ontario to the twentieth-century protagonist's quest for personal articulation and deeper cultural awareness. Margaret Laurence's use of the structure enables her to explore layers of historical experience, reveal inadequacies in the country's contemporary attitude to sub-cultures, and present a search for renewal that is both personal and collective.

The central figure is a forty-seven year old writer, Morag Gunn, who reviews her life during the early 1970s. When her eighteen year old daughter leaves home, she feels a middle-aged aloneness; she is induced to examine her life and the cultural values that have shaped it.

Her personal journey has been from a small town in Manitoba where she grew up. She travelled east and married an immigrant English professor; leaving him, she settled in the West; then she visited England and was particularly curious about Scotland whence her distant forbears had been expelled in the Clearances of the late eighteenth century; finally, seeking to "divine" her deepest self and its relationship to her culture, she settles down on a few acres of rural Ontario. These journeys have sharpened her awareness of personal growth and her society's formation but, in common with many of Patrick White's creations, the experience has left her with the sense of an irreducible mystery lying behind the development of all phenomena. Change, she concludes, is always multi-dimensional; when personal vision seems blocked by distress in one's private life or dismay at external social conditions, one must seek to restore the flow of perceptions by clarifying a new dimension; like a water-diviner one senses new life-sustaining sources by exploring beyond appearances. Morag finally resolves:

> Look ahead into the past, and back into the future, until the silence.[2]

The novel evokes aspects of Canada's complex cultural for-

mation. But instead of using negative retrospection or self-grati-
fying nostalgia as bases for the evocation, Laurence conducts a
vigorous assertive enquiry that examines the past in the hope of
contributing to a richer future. Her protagonist has lived through
some of the ethnic and class divisiveness that has vitiated Canada's
past and present. In addition, her daughter and lover have also suffered from the consequences of ethnic prejudice exercised by members of the dominant Anglophone culture. But the future, Morag
convinces herself, may be faced with an optimistic assertiveness.

She was raised by Christie Logan, a garbage collector of
Scots descent in a Manitoban small town. Almost two centuries
before, the Logans like other highland clans had been victimized
and dispossessed in their native Scotland. To survive they had been
compelled to acquire new vision and courage. When expelled from
the Scottish Sutherland estates the Logans, like Morag's own ancestors, had sought a new life in Canada. Their leader had been a piper
and his music gave hope to a people lost in despair; he and his music
nourished them on their journey to Northern Canada and on the
long march southwards. When the piper's resolution sometimes fal-
tered his woman, Morag, served to sustain him:

> *What in the fiery hell are we doing in this terrible place?* So Morag
> says to him for she had the wisdom and the good eye and
> the warmth of a home and the determination of quietness,
> and she says, *We are going into the new country and your child is
> going along with us, so play on.* And he did that (p. 85).

The terrible journey resumed; the immigrants' sufferings were
immense but their offspring grew to become part of Canadian society. Morag eagerly identifies with the heroic courage dramatized in
the tales of her ancestors.

The other major founding culture in the Canadian West is
that of the Metis. Part Indian, part Francophone, they had generally failed to gain the financial success and social status that some of

the Scots had achieved by the late nineteenth century. In Morag's childhood they were still the subjects of racial contempt in the Manitoban small town; and the stories of their incredible exploits, as courageous as any of the deeds of the Scots, were hidden away in private memories. Fascinated by language and by the power of narrative to invent and perpetuate values, Morag as a child began to uncover the Meti myths; she learned of the Tonnerre family who supported nineteenth-century rebellion both in Manitoba and Saskatchewan against the dominant Anglophone culture, of which the Scots had now become part. From young Jules Tonnerre, Morag discovered the heroism associated with the Meti journeys of protest and settlement across the West. She is shrewd enough to see that the stories she hears are sometimes contradictory, their factual bases long ago lost in fictional re-creations and their values deriving arbitrarily from the biases in the sub-culture of the narrators. A Meti like Jules Tonnerre would offer one version of events, a Scots Canadian like Christie Logan a very different account of the same incidents. But for Morag the facts are unimportant. By listening to the tales she is awakened to the magic of narration and perceives the absolute need for a people, when confronting a necessity that threatens their collective or cultural existence, to invent heroic fictions. Their stories disclose and perpetrate the founding values of their culture. In later life, Morag the novelist is to continue the process by constructing fictions that serve to define her personal experience and her Canadian identity.

Jules Tonnerre performs a similar function for his Meti sub-culture. He becomes a folk singer travelling the country singing about his people. His songs are tales of violence, early death, social repression and lost hopes; and his wandering life as a Meti singer brings him in regular contact with these traditional realities. The harrassment he experiences in his travels sharpens his myth-making capability; from poverty, disillusionment and distress his songs continue to come forth, articulating the past strength and present endurance of his Meti sub-culture.

In adult life Morag bears his child. As the young Pique grows up, she identifies more closely with her Meti ancestry: she inherits the yearning of her father and Meti forebears for restless travel. She also inherits her parents' fiction-making skills. As an eighteen year old she resolves to become an itinerant singer like her father and seek to spread positive, heroic myths that will help to confer dignity to her people.

One other person's journeying haunts the present and past consciousness of the middle-aged writer-mother Morag. While first settling in rural Ontario she recalls the person and books of the nineteenth-century English immigrant to the region Catharine Parr Traill. This gentlewoman from mannered English society, who struggled to adapt to the sometimes terrifying conditions of pioneering in the Ontario bush, wrote extensively of her experiences offering practical, and sometimes platitudinous, advice to other immigrants. Morag reflects on her and other pioneers:

> They *had* hacked out a living here. They had survived. Like so-called Piper Gunn and the Sutherlanders further West (p. 95).

But, on the whole, Morag can establish only a limited identification between her own twentieth-century journeying and the settlement journeying of the nineteenth-century woman. Each has confronted terror — Morag of increasing middle-aged loneliness and being forsaken by her adolescent daughter; Mrs. Traill, surrounded by seven children, had known the terror of the bush. Mrs. Traill's remedy was:

> In cases of emergency, it is folly to fold one's hand and sit down to bewail in abject terror: it is better to be up and doing (p. 406).

Morag's final understanding is similar: she appreciates the wisdom of action even when futility seems overwhelming — "the necessary doing of the thing — that mattered" (p. 452).

Her personal journeys, her discovery of the founding journeys of settlement and her deepened understanding of journeys related to ethnic conflict have exposed parts of Canada's cultural formation. The six journeys of *The Diviners* evoke the cultural evolution of two centuries and optimistically anticipate a future century when heroic myths will restore dignity to all victims of social prejudice. In Margaret Laurence's view, facts are less significant as a structuring force for bestowing dignity and changing entrenched attitudes than the fictions emerging from facts; these may act to heal social divisiveness and renew cultural possibilities. Journeys are at the centre of these optimistic narratives; but real journeys diminish in importance before the power of fictional, or mythic, journeys. At one point Laurence's protagonist Morag has the opportunity to visit Sutherland, the part of Scotland about which she has heard so much. But she stops some distance away, pausing to view the land from which her forbears had been expelled, and doesn't actually set foot on the soil. She explains to her host, a native Scot:

> "The myths are my reality ... I don't need to go there because I know now what it was I had to learn here ... I always thought it was the land of my ancestors, but it is not" (pp. 390-1).

Her "real land" is the myth of heroic journeying without which no new culture can be established.

(4)

In contrast to the replacement of factual journeying by mythic journeying, Euclides da Cunha in his Brazilian classic *Os Sertões* (1902) remains close to historical and geophysical fact in order to dramatize aspects of Brazilian cultural development. His childhood reading of the ancient Greek and Roman historians provided models for both the panoramic overview he offers and the narrative pace; his documentation is massive but its diverse parts are welded into a structure of masterly proportions. Known to the English-speaking world as *Rebellion in the Backlands*, the narrative seeks to separate recorded historical data from myth-making processes; essentially a narrative of flight and pursuit, it dramatizes the challenge offered by a dissident region under the leadership of a charismatic messiah to Brazilian federalism and cultural cohesiveness. Cunha's presentation of the sequence of historical journeys brilliantly exposes conflicts in Brazilian culture from its origins to the present.

The basic facts of the crisis are simple. In 1876 there appeared a backlands messiah named Antônio Conselheiro. He was at first only a small voice in the wilderness of the Brazilian North-East; but as he expressed social discontent and articulated the need for establishing a more just society, his followers increased. Finally he led them in open warfare against government forces. He proved himself a superb guerrilla fighter and the authorities required no less than four well-armed military expeditions in order to destroy him and his adherents. Although the latter showed absolute faith in their leader and displayed a matchless fighting heroism, they were finally killed one by one, in October 1897, during a persistent assault by the federal forces on their backlands stronghold.

Euclides da Cunha was by training a military engineer with an omnivorous appetite for knowledge. To the mass of factual details he had collected about Conselheiro and the personal experience gained from serving in the federal campaign against him, he brought a disciplined precision for organizing and dramatizing the opposing values in this military, political and cultural conflict. In *Os Sertões* he constructed a unique prose epic — an amalgam of basic facts, imaginative details and philosophic resonances — which is unparalleled in any other new-world literature.

He begins with an evocation of origins: regressing through time he offers an explorer's eye view of the sertões — the backlands of the Brazilian North-East. Barren and inhospitable, they were a region of profound poverty; nature seemed intolerantly cruel, making life impossible for the region's inhabitants. Yet Cunha's presentation goes beyond visual appearances and, like a contemporary ecologist, he sees the sources of the land's failure as human rather than natural. Intelligent engineering, he perceived, could irrigate the barrenness; with fertile soil, a large population could subsist. Asserting that "A natureza não cria normalmente os desertos" ("Nature does not normally create deserts"), he sees the area as still possessing a life-force — despite humanity's centuries-long ravages.

After making his geographical overview, Cunha conducts a historical survey to account for the region's sterility. Long ago the aboriginal Indians had systematically burnt off the primitive forest; as a consequence the soil gained a brief additional fertility; but the Indians exhausted that after a few short growing seasons and then moved on, burning over and planting larger and larger areas, transforming them into *caapuera* (extinct treeland). The barren areas became even more extensive when, in succeeding centuries, Portuguese colonisers and their African slaves followed the same procedure; but, unlike the Indians, the Europeans were motivated by huge commercial greed, not mere survival economics. They continued to devastate even vaster tracts which all became subject to soil erosion; and these *catas* seemed doomed to perpetual sterility.

So in Cunha's view of cultural formation, men made the desert as surely as they bestowed names on the territory. And they were comparably adept in making a desert of human consciousness; missionaries established a hold over the racially mixed sertanejos by preaching a gospel of fear and damnation. Their stern teachings combined with the inhabitants' prolonged physical deprivation to breed fanaticism; one form this took was turning inward away from the environmental barrenness to excesses of personal penitential flagellation. But the same fanaticism could also turn outwards and confer faith on a charismatic leader, especially one who promised to better the squalid, seemingly irremediable, condition of his follow-

ers. From such poverty of environment and spirit Antônio Conselheiro derived his strength and power.

Euclides da Cunha introduces the man with a geological
metaphor that suggests his natural outgrowth from the region's
geophysical and ethnic reality:

> É natural que estas camadas profundas da nossa estratifica-
> ção étnica se sublevassem numa anticlinal extraordinária —
> Antônio Conselheiro . . . [3]

> It was natural the deep-lying layers of our ethnic stratifica-
> tion should have cast up an anticlinal so extraordinary as
> Antônio Conselheiro.

But having been thus cast up, Antônio followed in the local tradition
of penitential preaching by adapting to his own purposes its crude
systematization of rewards and penalties; quickly he took on the
aura of prophet, messiah and millenarian leader. His appeal was to
victims of social neglect and regional discrimination. As he gave the
landless sertanejos a sense of human dignity, his criticisms of their
condition inevitably took on a political aspect. When he objected to
paying taxes, he began preaching open insurrection against the local government; the authorities responded by sending troops to
rout the dissidents. But Antônio's followers won the day. This happened over and over, and the details of flight, regroupment, pursuit
and assault structure Cunha's detailed factual narrative.

The army's final march is against the dissident community
of Canudos, a township Antônio had established and fortified for
his followers. There they had achieved a firm social bonding; they
had become an autonomous sect, austere, self-punishing, utterly
committed to their own values and subservient to their counsellor-
leader:

> Áceitando, às cegas, tudo quanto lhe ensinara aquêle;

imersa de todo no sonho religioso; vivendo sob a preocupa-
ção doentia da outra vida, resumia o mundo na linha de
serranias que a cingiam. Não cogitava de instituições garan-
tidoras de um destino na Terra.

Eram-lhe inúteis. Canudos era o cosmos . . .

Nada queriam desta vida . . .

De tôdas as páginas de catecismo que soletrara ficara-lhe
preceito único: *Bem-aventurados os que sofrem* . . . (p. 142)

Accepting blindly all that this man taught them, com-
pletely immrsed in a religious dream, living only with the
melancholy obsession of a future life, they made their world
behind a protective line of mountains that surrounded
them. There was no thought of establishing institutions that
might guarantee them a human life here on the earth.

That was a meaningless concept. For Canudos was their
cosmos . . .

They wished for nothing from this life . . .

Of all the catechism's pages that he preached the one pre-
cept constantly stressed was: "Blessed are those that suffer."

The twenty-year conflict, so important for Brazil's cultural
development had, in Cunha's view, an economic dimension. An immeasurable gap had grown between the settled civilization of the
seaboard, where federal power was entrenched, and the absolute
pauperization of the backlands. In the former region a new and
prosperous society was being born from immigration, settlement
and urbanization. Ideals of self-improvement were transforming
and enriching the population, offering promises of boundless
growth and individual happiness. In contrast the vast sertões of the
North-East offered few ideals; and the grim reality of ecological ravishment and general misdevelopment had produced a society that
was both stagnant and resentful. There was a strong heritage of
authoritarian rule by religious and civic leaders; and upon this tradition, dissident leaders like Antônio Conselheiro could appeal to

their followers and rapidly gain a massive following.

From the federal viewpoint, Antônio's rebellion was a challenge not only to regional government but also to the newly instituted system of federalism; unless checked, other areas could resist central government and seek to form autonomous regions.

The clash of values and attitudes permitted no easy resolution. In effect, Antônio's leadership brought into existence a powerful sub-culture fuelled by resentment and self-righteousness. By describing this opposition with a wealth of analysis, Euclides da Cunha transforms a simple narrative of rebellion, flight and pursuit into an elaborate cultural epic. The journeys take on heroic proportions. The battles become ferocious constituents in the birth of a nation. Although his loyalties are with federal values, Cunha understands the injustices suffered through centuries by the people of the sertões; he saw that the gap separating them from the people of the seaboard could not be bridged and was actually increasing; but his remarkable narrative shows that, as an engineer, he glimpsed the social amelioration that can come from forms of conscious cultural engineering. Such was the distinctive insight he dramatized in *Os Sertões*.

(5)

Different in style and purpose is the richly complex account of journeying to the South American heartland described in Alejo Carpentier's *Los pasos perdidos (The Lost Steps)* first published in 1953. It is one of the most profound of the new-world narratives that seek to expose layers of indigenous cultural experience concealed beneath historical time and imposed European values. Some details about Alejo Carpentier help to explain this major exploration of South American culture.

He was born in Cuba and, as a young man, like many other Hispanic Americans travelled to Paris seeking both intellectual roots and a sense of his artistic identity. But by the late 1930s he was disillusioned, sensing that Europe was on the verge of another war. He returned to the new world and, a few years later, received an invitation to travel into the interior of Venezuela. He was attracted to the proposal as he wanted to gain a more immediate contact with the vast rivers, plains and mountains of the mainland. He journeyed to the upper reaches of the Orinoco, lived a month with prehistoric tribal bands and, while keeping a journal of his experiences, thought of composing a travel-book. However he transformed his material into a novel and *Los pasos perdidos* became one of the seminal works of modern South American fiction. The documentary details of geography, regional history and ethnography combine with the authentic personal experience to produce an epic prose-poem comparable to *Os Sertões*.

Carpentier's search, like that of his unnamed protagonist, was for cultural continuity. If a common strand could be discerned between tribal people, colonizing people, proselytizing people, revolutionary people, dictatorial people and twentieth-century ordinary people, then the processes that have contributed to the making of South America could be brought together into a meaningful cultural whole. But he sensed that currently there was only diversity and incommunication of values:

> "piense que nosotros, por tradición, estamos acostumbrados a ver convivir Rousseau con el Santo Oficio, y los pendones al emblema de la Virgen con *El Capital* . . . "[4]

> "I would say that traditionally we're accustomed to see living side by side Rousseau and the Holy Inquisition, the banners on the Virgin's picture together with *Das Kapital* . . . "

The speaker is a lawyer in a remote interior town; his ironic observation seems to express with humourous evocativeness Crpentier's own cultural perspectives on the South American continent:

America es el único continente donde distintas edades coexisten, donde un hombre del siglo veinte puede darse la mano con otro del Cuaternario o con otro de poblados sin periódicos ni communicaciones que se asemeja al de la Edad Media o existir contemporáneamente con otro de provincia más cerca de romanticismo de 1850 que de esta época.[5]

South America is the only continent where distinct ages coexist, where a man from the twentieth century can take the hand of someone from the fourteenth century; or the hand of someone from a society without newspapers or communications living in a mediæval style; or he can live contemporaneously with some provincial personality closer to the romanticism of 1850 than to this age.

So Carpentier has his unnamed narrator in *Los pasos perdidos* undertake a journey to explore this colossal disjunctive diversity that spreads through past time and present reality.

As a young man, the fictional hero, like Carpentier, had first tried to find cultural continuity and personal identity by travelling to Europe. His genetic roots were in the old world: his musician father had migrated from Europe but always retained in his new culture a distrust for the continent to which he had come. For him it was a land of savagery, devoid of social balance and the traditions manufactured by conscious history. Raised with this paternal bias in favour of the old world, the narrator had strong longings to see Europe for himself.

But his youthful encounter with the highly civilized continent had brought only distress. The period was the 1930s and the heirs of Beethoven and Calderón were actively preparing to engage in war. The continent that had produced the ideas, technology and social energy to settle the Americas was entering a new barbarism — embarking on a bloodletting that not even the long Mexican wars of the early twentieth century could equal. So to the young protagonist

Europe has come to suggest broken, maimed and twisted images —
the Grotescas of Goya rather than the physical harmonies of
Michelangelo.

At the start of *Los pasos perdidos* he has returned to the new
world realizing that cultural origins and continuity must be found
there and not among the dead bones of Europe. He first lived in a
North American metropolis, possibly New York City, where he experienced a vacuous theatricality of daily living: he felt that existence among the anonymous crowds was only a performance — an
imitation and reiteration of living — presented before an unknown
audience until every word and gesture had become meaningless.
His very being became meaningless as a consequence.

Then, when a museum gives him the opportunity to make
an expedition to the South American interior in search of native
musical instruments, he leaves the labyrinthine reality of North
American urban life and journeys southwards into the little-known
heartland.

His travels enable him to encounter the enormous richness
of his South American heritage — the cumulative experience of different centuries living contemporaneously side by side: modern
revolution and urban violence coexisted with life-styles belonging to
the time of European Discovery and Conquest; mediæval Europe
still asserted itself in the perpetuation of religious liturgies that controlled a subject populace; and behind all this lay the inescapable
reality of Palaeolithic humanity surviving unchanged and uncon-
quered in the jungles. One encounter after another discloses to him
the frightening fact that South American society does not possess
one cohesive value system, but multiple, coexisting and contradictory systems. The protagonist's journey, like Carpentier's, becomes
an experience and celebration of diverse and irreconcilable values.

Finally, hidden deep in the jungle, in a small pre-Columbian
native community, which also includes several modern dropouts
and a watchful catholic priest, he finds a culture that contrasts stark-
ly with the impersonal urban values of North America that had pro-

voked in him such dissatisfaction. Community rhythms and values begin to infiltrate his being; his sense of time changes; he becomes unconcerned about possessions and does not live in fretful fear of the future. He discovers a renewal of joy in daily living.

But more than finding this inward spiritual happiness is the incentive to examine basic assumptions that have shaped his previous thinking and perceiving. Because he had previously earned his living as a composer of film music, he had pondered as a minor creative artist the origins of sound, music, words. He had inherited the Greek philosophic answers to the origin of art — that it is an imitation of Nature which becomes an object of contemplation capable of elevating human responses to transcendent levels. Now he begins to understand that part of the deadness he attributes to modern art derives from the European assumption about mimesis. What is sanctified as imitation has led to the invention of the proscenium arch separating art from nature, function from ritual, content from symbol and, ultimately, people from art. Subdivision into meaningless units is the end consequence of this particular European assumption. It is the death of authentic culture. This was the death he had experienced in North American urban living.

One day he witnesses the actions of the tribal shaman around the body of a hunter killed by a rattlesnake. The shaman shakes a gourd of pebbles; members of the band gather — watchful. Then two voices issue from the shaman — one similar to the dead man's speech comes from his throat and the other, representing the dead man's spirit, issues from the shaman's belly. The voices interact in harsh counterpoint, changing pitch, forming rhythms, making trills and forming the embryo of a melody.

The narrator understands suddenly that he witnesses something which is neither language nor song; more terrible and wonderful, it is the Birth of Music. He realizes that the origin of art is not reclusive, contemplative and elitist, as the aristocratic European imagination had assumed for centuries; instead it is born of community and social interaction which, in moments of personal or collective peril, is formalized into ritual. The birth of art is therefore the result of humanity's confrontation with necessity. In the face of death, the community asserts its own patterns of order, shapes its own culture, as sound, music, words, symbols and rituals are consciously patterned to repel the rapacious intrusion of unknown menace. And living with the constant awareness of necessity makes creation continuous and cultural effort a daily, magical utterance.

But Carpentier does not postulate a simple Romantic primitivism. He understands that a twentieth-century artist cannot return to past styles of making and that he is indissolubly bound to the culture that shaped him. Carpentier does not leave his protagonist to be absorbed by the jungle community. The shaman is able to make art by sounds from his throat and belly; but the twentieth-century artist, his consciousness shaped in an age of print, needs paper. So he must return to a culture based on paper if he is to express his perceptions. And there, with his sensitivity freshly alerted by his journeying, he is likely to remain.

The protagonist's travels have enabled him to experience the values that have contributed to his culture. He has journeyed to the culture's roots and made a radical analysis of its assumptions; he saw clearly its predispositions and peered into the nature of creativity and life itself. Consequently, he can never again be content with any form of imitation; he must dedicate himself to exploring and discovering all values for himself and never remain satisfied with imposed, tradition-honoured assumptions from the old world that narrow the immense possibilities of new-world perception. He must live the rest of his life in the new perspectives that radical analysis, stimulated by his journeying, has opened up to him. His search for cultural continuity — for ordering the multiple, coexisting and contradictory value-systems of South America — becomes a daily necessity from which an art worthy of the new world will be born. The protagonist's journey, begun in disillusion, has concluded in affirmation.

Summary

The narrative device of journeying enables new-world writers to develop a radical analysis of their culture. Dramatizing a personal or collective crisis initially reveals the structuring values that
have hitherto sustained social behavioral patterns; the crisis neces-
sarily provokes the search — the journeying to define — alternative
values, perspectives and life-attitudes. However the crisis may be
finally resolved, the knowledge derived by the conclusion of the exploratory journeying offers a potential for amending the value-system and strengthening the culture.

The fictionalized journeys, which may present historical
episodes or persons, usually dramatize cultural divisiveness; but as
the journey unfolds, the narrative offers, or implies to various degrees, the potential for a healing integration of the disjunctive diversity within the dominant culture. Perhaps the most radical and
Romantic presentations of exploratory journeying are by the classic
United States writers Melville and Twain; but even Melville's Ishma-
el must return to shore and reintegrate with a culture at some time,
and Twain's Huck Finn cannot "light out" for his imagined territory
all his life. Essentially the device of journeying enables a writer to
offer an overview of his culture, bringing multi-ethnic values and
sub-cultural attitudes into focus.

Alejo Carpentier described the process at the time he was
completing *Los pasos perdidos*. Writing and re-writing the book, he
states, helped him to find his "American accent." This was in part
the discovery of "a continent where one of the most extraordinary
cultural events of history took place, since it became the crossroads
in which, for the first time, races that had never met found each
other".[6] But more intimately it was an artistic awareness of the life
the artist "must lead in a continent subject to different telluric
forces, that offers him new scales of distance, a new table of propor-

tions between man and the landscape." The narrative device of journeying bridges the enormous gap between the external socio-historical phenomena that shaped the culture and the artist's inward vision seeking to encompass new proportions. Until new scales of spiritual distance have been established, the culture may remain in a state of arid imitativeness, as the protagonist in *Los pasos perdidos* discovered; it will continue to draw upon proportions and cultural values that derive from alien societies. The work of Patrick White in Australia, Margaret Laurence in Canada, Euclides da Cunha and Alejo Carpentier in South America represent the search to clarify new proportions and chart new distances. The poetry of Walt Whitman, the frontier narratives of Mark Twain and the epic grandeur of William Carlos Williams are similar efforts to identify and articulate unique cultural proportions. Carpentier's "new scales of distance" are comparable to Whitman's and Williams' search for a new measure; the journey of Carpentier's protagonist is similar to the wide-eyed cultural criticism embodied in Twain's wandering Huckleberry Finn. The narrative device of journeying enables a perspective based on new proportions that are more appropriate for the new culture to be tentatively established and explored.

1. White, *Voss* (New York, 1957), p. 36.
2. Laurence, *The Diviners* (New York, 1974), p. 453.
3. Cunha, *Os Sertões* (Rio de Janeiro, 1968), p. 111.
4. Carpentier, *Los Pasos Perdidos* (Mexico, 1966), p. 56.
5. Giacomin, *Homenaje a Alejo Carpentier* (New York, 1970), pp. 107-8.
6. Echeverría, *Alejo Carpentier: The Pilgrim at Home* (Ithaca, 1977), p. 188.

Chapter Four

PROCESSES: FAMILY STRUCTURE

Hambre, coral del hombre

Pablo Neruda

(1)

All new societies upset pre-existing psycho-social arrangements. Assumptions about gender relationship and rationalizations
about inter-gender responsibility were challenged by the movement
of people from old to new societies. Immigrants and their offspring
inaugurated change, the indigenous population endured change;
and no one could foresee the full generational consequences of the
new patterns of relationship. Pioneers, convicts, indentured labourers, militiamen, slaves, free immigrants and native peoples
were all caught up in psycho-social arrangements which had no pri-
or models in their original cultures. Religious, ethnic and class inter-
breeding together with divorce, homoeroticism, the collapse of the
christian monogamous nuclear family, and new behavioral patterns
assumed by the extended family may all have been restrained or
prevented in the former societies; but, impelled by an innate restlessness, new cultures forced realignments of gender roles and relationships. Thus the prohibited became generationally more nor-
mal; and, as the process continued, the latest conventions in new
societies were exported to the older countries, both alarming and
reanimating their populations with values traditionally forbidden.

The same restless surge and critical discontent with conditions in the home countries which made immigrants of simple citizens overflowed, after the trials of settlement, into a dynamic of
change that contributed to the rhythmic lifeforce of a new society.
Often the urge to experiment is embodied by the original immigrants' children and their offspring. Where this principle is denied

or perverted by adherence to "rigidities" often imported from older cultures, social degradation and cultural stagnation invariably result. The problem for the family nexus, seeking to survive and contain vast changes, is twofold: how to accept, define and mediate meaningful change within the family; secondly, no matter what personal or family successes are achieved, how to adjust to the psychosocial experience of the new society.

No abstract values can be imported to frontier, or post-frontier, regions without undergoing dilution. Despite centuries-long assertions to the contrary, the same iron law applies to religious systems. Religious organization, the major preserver of traditional family order, fails to retain unchanged its own traditional values; as a consequence of this diminished state, it also fails to continue exercising control over the values structuring family units. Thus, the nuclear family, that benign, constrictive invention of mediæval christianity, together with the extended family systems endorsed by oriental religions, both suffer internal change and subtle disintegration before the exigencies of life in new territories.

Changes in national or regional behaviour become filtered through the family nexus. This mediation is particularly difficult for, without the abstract values perpetuated as "eternal", "revealed" or "god-given" by religious disciplines in old-world societies, the family nexus itself in new societies must continually seek to define consistent values. Within the surge and restlessness of the culture, it tries, but usually fails, to facilitate personal adjustment to externally generated change. But it must additionally function to mediate internal changes within its own structure, sometimes endorsing, sometimes repudiating, but generally inventing norms for accepting or judging the behaviour of its members.

We shall look at four major novels, each of which reveals its culture's predispositions, to see how the narratives dramatize family relationships mediating changes that are generated within the family or in the culture itself.

Perhaps the most successful transfer of European ideals about family structure to the new world was from Catholic France in the seventeenth and eighteenth centuries to rural Quebec. There, in a fragment of North America, the twin concepts of life-long monogamy and the family as society's indissoluble basic unit were implemented by clerical administrators who had divided the territory into tightly-knit parishes. Each parish lay under the immediate supervision of a priest who was, in turn, responsible to superior church administrators. His status among the *habitant* farmers and small-town bourgeoisie was high and unchallengeable. He and the church authority supporting him were more powerful in local communities than secular government. When in the nineteenth century, after the separation of Quebec from France, British administrators were reorganizing the North American territories into a new nation-state, their constitutional efforts and ideals had less influence on the Francophone rural populace than that possessed by the parish priest and the hierarchy of the Quebec church. Any ideas or attitudes that might challenge or offer alternative values to parishioners were carefuly deflected by the clerical power elite, so that the *habitant,* surviving on his farm by hard lifelong struggle, continued to accept the one value-system promulgated by church authority. One consequence of this total control was a high level of social stability; but another effect was intellectual and cultural stagnation. So vast was the latter that change, when it finally came through economic forces and innovative technology, swept over a people unprepared for the making of social adjustments. To many *habitants* the time-tested order their ancestors had known seemed the only possible, god-ordained system.

Ringuet's novel *Trente arpents* (1938) exposes in brilliant balanced contrasts the strengths and weakness of rural Quebec's traditional social order. Its straightforward narrative employs a complex irony to bring out the lights and shades of relationship within an *habitant* family surviving on the land through several generations.

The central figure is Euchariste Moisan who, around the turn of the twentieth century, at the age of twenty-two, inherits from his uncle, a childless widower, a farm of thirty acres. The inheritance is a mixed beneficence. On the one hand Euchariste feels exhilarated at owning a part of the Quebec soil — *his* piece of the earth; on the other hand, receiving the land ties him to the customs of the land and a traditional style of life.

Acquiring property makes him eligible for marriage. He looks on this prospect without any romantic idealizing; or, in Ringuet's phrase, Euchariste does not clothe his favoured Alphonsine with the garb of the madonna. Instead he calculates the benefits obtainable from the union with cautious precision:

> De visage avenant, bien tournée de sa personne, elle lui donnerait des gars solides après des plaisirs auxquels il pensait sans honte ni hâte exagérée.[1]

> She had a pleasant face and a satisfactory figure; and, after enjoying those physical pleasures which he anticipated without guilt or undue haste, she would produce healthy children.

There is an inevitability about the whole family-making process: "Et puisqu'il fallait que ça se fasse . . . autant maintenant que plus tard" (p.19). ("And since it had to happen, just as well now as later.") Marriage and procreation are the human part of the natural processes of seeding and harvesting:

> Il allait récolter plus que jamais n'avait semé son imagination contenue par les bornes étroites de l'habitude (p. 27).

> He was going to reap more than his imagination, so constricted by the tight bonds of custom, had ever sown.

Euchariste's inheritance of the thirty acres now becomes a shared possession; Alphonsine takes over the farm-house and is able to speak of "our fields". But full possession of the land comes to each only when Alphonsine grows pregnant. Then the quality of being a "stranger" — each to the land, and one to the other — which has characterized the first months of their marriage, disappears for ever. Procreation grants Euchariste a new sense of mastery over the land and offers him a glimpse of his ancestral past in which generations of *habitants* like himself tilled the Quebec earth.

In effect, he gains a new perspective on time; now, like his forebears, by sharing in procreation, he can date events from within a family structure; no longer a "stranger", he can look from inside the protective wall of his family; as a more secure "insider" he now looks outward to measure events in the external world.

Alphonsine has also progressed from being "strange" to both man and farm; having become a wife she shares in the farm's material possessions. But she achieves her full human status, equivalent to Euchariste's "possession" of the land, only after delivering her first child. For in this rural catholic value-system her primary role is mother, and not wife. After delivery, the energy-flow of the family is re-directed:

> Euchariste: les champs; Alphonsine: la maison et l'enfant. La vie passait de la terre à l'homme, de l'homme à la femme, et de la femme à l'enfant qui était le terme temporaire (p. 56).

> Euchariste tended the fields, Alphonsine the house and the child. The life-force passed from the land to the man, from the man to the woman, and from the woman to the child, the present end-recipient.

By completing the link in the energy chain, each partakes in an order of family living that is both traditional and fundamental. The man receives sustenance from the female earth and also from the mother church; he supports the mother of his children; and the offspring, with the passing of time, will support him and continue the family. Such is the poetic-metaphysical structure of the agrarian family relationship.

But reality shows the inadequacy of this cultural perspective. Dependence on the female earth provides an insecure basis for human life: the land may be prodigal or meagre, benevolent or resistant and the family can only enjoy or endure the consequences. The human mother was enjoined to be always prodigal. Large numbers of children demonstrated her womanliness and spiritual closeness to the sources of life; but continual childbearing also debilitated her and, in Ringuet's ironic portrayal, promoted a passivity that gently eased Alphonsine into a premature death. At the age of forty, after twenty years of childbearing, she died giving birth to her thirteenth child.

By her death the unity of the family is damaged from within. Further disruptions follow. Although the thirty-acre strip of land was able to nourish all the children, when grown up they had to find alternative sources of economic support. Traditionally, daughters had married local farmers; some of the sons had travelled to Northern Quebec, bringing the harsher land under the plough, or working in logging camps; others had gone to live in big Canadian cities and some had emigrated to the factory system of the United States.

Ringuet shows these influences affecting rural Quebec; some of them invade the Moisan family. The force of twentieth-century change is so great that no family — even in isolated, over-protected, rural Quebec — can remain separate from it. Although the traditional family was able to mediate internal changes, such as the death of a parent or the departure of grownup children, it was unable to adapt easily to rapid technological change. Ringuet focuses on two sons, Etienne and Ephrem, to dramatize changes in family structure for the generation succeeding Euchariste.

As a young man, Etienne intrigues to take over the thirty

acres for this own family. As Euchariste ages, Etienne engages on a "methodical usurpation" to displace his father and finally drives out the old man. But having become possessor of the land, he also is doomed like Euchariste to age and show a lack of adaptability to external change. After managing the property successfully for more than a decade and raising his own children, he is shown in the ironic final sequence of the novel petulantly resisting his son's suggestions for raising alternate crops. The young Etienne impatient with his father's reluctance to change has become the older man demonstrating, like Euchariste, a similar inability to adapt.

His brother Ephrem had chosen emigration to the United States and, after Etienne takes over the farm, his father joins him. There Euchariste lives a sterile, mechanical existence. His relationships to the land and to a recognizable family structure are gone. He now lives surrounded by industrial pollution and new psycho-social attitudes.

The aged Euchariste is amazed that Ephrem has only two children, that his wife is not totally dedicated to household and child-tending duties, and that the family, in effect, is more open to external social and economic influences than it was in the more protected system of his native Quebec. His son is not able to look outwards upon events from within the family structure, as he had been able; instead Ephrem, like others in technological society, looks from external conditions inwards towards his own family.

In effect, neither family nor church are powerful enough to mediate change. Family members become, in the United States' industrialized culture, isolated individuals; each is responsible for his own behaviour and each is part of a vast impersonal pattern of socio-economic forces. From these little protection is possible. Money determines relationships, local politicians give out jobs, adultery is a mode of self-advancement, children exploit parents and the economic depression of the 1930s threatens all. Old Euchariste feels he has left family and community for a meagre existence in a large barracks.

Trente arpents presents both the perpetuation and disintegration of the traditional family structure in rural Quebec. Despite its member's poor education and hard life-long toil, the family offered protection and a poetic-religious vision of human existence which enriched their lives and enabled them to look from the security of the family outwards to external conditions. But Ringuet saw also the inadequacies of the system and judged its inability to mediate change, especially that generated by United States' technology. Perhaps he saw that before such awesome power no mediation was possible. The traditional family was inevitably caught up in processes that were to change psycho-social values and inter-gender relationships. The old-world family structure that had survived for several centuries in rural Quebec would still survive but in an attenuated state and with the loss of many of its members. The new-world dynamic of change prevailed.

(3)

Graciliano Ramos' narrative study of a landless peasant family in the Brazilian backlands *Vidas Sêcas (Barren Lives)* was published in 1938, the same year as Ringuet's *Trente arpents*. Although each portrays the strategies of family survival, the impact of the external society on family members and the parental dreams of family continuity, the difference in cultural values dramatized by the two narratives is vast. To move from the established modest rural prosperity of the land-owning Quebec *habitant* to the bare world of the landless Brazilian backlander is to enter a consciousness and culture in which, unlike Quebec, personal rights are few, the impoverished are many, legal justice is uncertain and the authoritarian power of local landowners is limitless and arbitrary. Although each culture was structured on values originating in the Roman Catholic church, the resultant social realities are widely different.

Despite limitations on behaviour that is contrary to the traditional value-system, Euchariste Moisan and his family cherish the land they own, feel that their patch of the Quebec earth is part of a rich Quebec heritage, and act as responsible and responsive individuals within their social nexus. They possess the capability of making their dreams for a better life come true; they shape their own destiny with a distinctive optimism that belongs to the North American continent.

On the other hand, Fabiano, Vitória and their two sons in *Vidas Sêcas* represent the countless numbers who, in impoverished agriculture-based economies throughout South America, are unable to eke a family subsistence from the land; and so they wander the countryside, seeking temporary employment, dreaming of a permanent home, and frequently ending up as migrants to the overcrowded cities.

Ramo's title, *Vidas Sêcas,* implies that the dry land produces dry, or barren, human lives. He initially dramatizes the plight of such people by showing Fabiano and Vitória's family struggling to survive in the midst of drought. Under famine conditions in the immense Brazilian North-East, they have been forced to kill and eat the family pet — a parrot. The act was comparable to killing a human member of the family. But they chew the parrot's scrawny flesh with relish and their dog gnaws at his former companion's bones. Still hungry, the two adults fight to assert a will to live against encroaching lethargy. Husband and wife succour each other:

> Miudinhos, perdidos no deserto queimado, os fugitivos agarraram-se, somaram as suas desgraças e os seus pavores. O coraçao de Fabiano bateu junto do coraçao de sinha Vitória, um abraço cansado aproximou os farrapos que os cobriam. Resistiram à fraqueza, afastaram-se envergonhados, sem ânimo de afrontar de novo a luz dura, receosos de perder a esperança que os alentava.[2]

Tiny and lost in the burning desert, the wanderers clutched at one another, sharing their misfortunes and fears. Fabiano's heart beat next to Vitória's; a tired embrace joined the rags that covered them. They resisted the impulse; they drew apart, ashamed, lacking the energy to confront the hard light again, and fearful of losing the hope that nurtured them.

The positive action, in this instance an impulse to physical love, is followed by negative emotion and negative attitudes. Fabiano and Vitória have no easy access to hope or optimism; and they live, with their young sons, in a common negative defensive life-posture that Ramos implies is typical of the landless peasant family.

His descriptive term is the traditional word *destino*. His protagonists' characters and general quality of life were determined by birth:

> Nascera com esse destino, ninguém tinha culpa de ele haver nascido com um destino ruim. Que fazer? Podia mudar a sorte? Se lhe dissessem que era possível melhorar de situação espantar-se-ia . . . Conformava-se, não pretendia mais nada. Se lhe dessem o que era dele, estava certo. Não davam. Era um desgraçado, era como um cachorro, só recebia ossos (pp. 161-2).

> He was born to his fate; no one was guilty for his having been born to a harsh fate. What could he do? Could he change fate? If anyone told him it was possible to change his fate, he would be astounded . . . He accepted the given situation, he didn't ask for more. If only they would give what was due him life was bearable. But they didn't. He was a fated fellow; he was like a dog, so what he got was bones.

Fabiano's acceptance of humble employment, lowly status and class injustice has typified not only his own attitude but also that of his forebears. All their lives were filled with self-negation, social submissiveness and acceptance of family responsibility in the face of adverse circumstances.

As Fabiano assumes he cannot change circumstances, the most he can do for his family is offer a protective wall built from his own endeavours. He tries to provide for wife and children within that wall — although, because his best efforts are often inadequate, they are required to contribute additionally as best they can. A pattern of negative family supportiveness is established; and, because Fabiano possesses no mode of intervening in external society, two consequences follow from this attitude.

First, whenever he ventures outside the protective wall and apart from his family, he loses self-confidence, tends to behave foolishly and always ends by accepting the will of a person — such as policeman or landowner — who is more socially dominant than himself. And so the pattern of personal negative submissiveness is reinforced.

Secondly, Fabiano remains enclosed within his private, non-communicative consciousness. He talks little; his sons are still young enough to be curious and question him about the external world, but Fabiano is content with not knowing and not speaking. Although he respects knowledge he has a large distrust of it. His recurrent dream is to possess his own patch of land; an alternate dream is his fantasy of having the freedom of a bandit to exercise power over others. But his fantasy is futile, his misgivings large, and Fabiano remains locked in the tight circle of his personal consciousness, unable to mediate the external world on behalf of his family.

While he acts as silent sturdy provider, responsibility for mediation falls upon Vitória. She protects the children when they are bewildered and afraid; she has the domestic dream of a permanent home; she has the energy to try to change Fabiano's fixed attitude by urging him to abandon a life of herding in the backlands for a better life on the plains or, if that fails, in the city beyond. At first Fabiano dismisses her promptings:

O optimismo de sinha Vitória ja não lhe fazia mossa. Ela

ainda se agarrava a fantasias. Coitada. Armar semelhantes planos, assim bamba, o peso do baú e da cabeça enterrando-lhe o pescoço no corpo (p. 205).

These days Vitória's optimism had little effect on him. She was just clinging to dreams, a silly woman. To make plans like she did when the weight of the suitcase and the water-gourd was pressing her neck down into her shoulders.

But her seemingly ridiculous dreams prevail not only over him but also over the children. She devises a way by which the older boy carries the water-gourd; in the delicate symbolism of Ramos' narrative this suggests both a new sharing of family responsibility and a more satisfying life for all when new attitudes have been adopted. Finally she is able to induce Fabiano to overcome his misgivings about unknown regions; he curbs his distrust of schools and learning, and heads his family towards the city. He gains the deceptive security of a positive goal:

As palavras de sinha Vitória encantavam-no. Iriam para diante, alcançariam uma terra desconhecida. Fabiano estava contente e acreditava nessa terra, porque não sabia como ela era nem onde era. Repetia dòcilmente as palavras de sinha Vitória, as palavras que sinha Vitória murmurava porque tinha confiança nele. E andavam para o sul, metidos naquele sonho (pp. 210-11).

Vitória's words enchanted him. They would go forward, they would come to an unknown land. Fabiano was content; he trusted in that land because he didn't know what it was like or where it was. Docilely he repeated Vitória's words — the words she kept on murmuring because she trusted in him, her husband. And they walked on southwards, surrounded by their dream.

In effect the restlessness of new-world society, operating through Vitória, overtakes and revitalizes the family. Her insistence on leaving their customary environment animates Fabiano and provides motivations that must influence the children. Instead of repeating the pattern characteristic of traditional societies in which, generation after generation, the children take on the parents' attitudes, tasks and responsibilities, Fabiano's and Vitória's family moves to an uncertain future and unknown life-time tasks. Rather than accept the sterile necessity imposed by inequitable social conditions and an adverse environment, they go forth — after surviving the ravages of drought, famine, hard toil, meagre pay and subsistence living — to create their own necessity. Inevitably they will acquire new values and, in the turbulence of change, passivity and submissiveness — even in so stolid, conservative and lethargic a person as Fabiano — must become infused with Vitória's optimistic vigour. Although the changes may appear small and as delicate as the symbolism of exchanging the water-gourd, they are in fact fundamental; there is small likelihood that the two sons, in their manhood either on the plains or in the city, would establish family values similar to their parents'.

In the final sentences Ramos makes explicit the type-figures he has been portraying:

> Chegariam a uma terra desconhecida e civilizada, ficariam presos nela. E o sertão continuaria a mandar gente para lá. O sertão mandaria para a cidade homens fortes, brutos, como Fabiano, sinha Vitória e os dois meninos (p. 211).

> They would come to an unknown and civilized land; they would be imprisoned by it. And the backlands would continue to send people there. The backlands would send to the civilized city strong, honest, uncouth, unformed people like Fabiano, Vitória and the two sons.

Ramos' expectation, unlike that of Ringuet whose protagonists are threatened with loss of language and culture by transference to urban living, is that his backlanders will acquire more "civilized" values and strategies for survival amid the hustle, exploitation and general experience of the city. To seize one's fate and create one's necessity in the dymanics of a new-world city will challenge family cohesiveness; but, in Ramos' view, from the new parameters of limitation and freedom, more civilized persons and inter-relationships will emerge.

(4)

Patrick White's *The Tree of Man* (1956) dramatizes values belonging to a tradition of sturdy protestantism. The value-system endorsed by protestantism generated courage in persons suffering the isolation of individualist pioneering. Much of the novel focuses on the survival of one pioneering family in the Australian bush. The period covered by the narration is approximately the same as that surveyed in Ringuet's *Trente arpents*. But in almost every other respect the narratives differ.

Stan Parker, the protagonist of *The Tree of Man,* comes alone to the empty bush. Unlike Euchariste Moisan he has no forebears who have broken in the land by generations of tillage, no community to lessen his aloneness, and no metaphysical sense of belonging to nature and the land; nor has he any established religious system, with social entrenchments, to which as he grows older he may refer his unanswerable questions about the meaning of life.

Patrick White writes out of a tradition of protestantism which exalts the efforts of individuals to find their own enlightenment; no absolutist church exists offering a single value-system and integrating its assertions into language that shapes popular consciousness as in Quebec, Brazil and major Spanish-speaking countries. Instead, religion is a peripheral phenomenon which an individual brings to the centre of his personal consciousness as and when he chooses. White's reiterated theme in novel after novel shows the necessity and inevitability of such a process within any person who tries to sustain an authentic inner development. But White is acutely aware that, in the absence of a single institutionalized religious system, the price of spiritual growth is loneliness; and in *The Tree of Man* he makes subtle analogues between the emptiness of the bush and the emptiness of the pioneer's life. Stan Parker asks the human unanswerable questions but there is no other person or organization able to respond:

> If a poetry sometimes almost formed in his head, or a vision of God, nobody knew, because you did not talk about such things, or, rather, you were not aware of the practice of doing so.[3]

Silence marks his deepest life and also characterizes his family's life. After first breaking in the bush and building a crude home, Stan marries and brings Amy as his wife to the isolated settlement. Constrained by poverty and schooled to expect little, Amy coped with the rigours of pioneering; but her profoundest wish is for a child. Unfortunately, after several years of marriage, her first attempt to give birth ends in failure; and this casts its shadow over all her future life.

She finally delivers two children — Ray and Thelma. She lavishes her maternal love on the son who grows, as a township develops around them, into a moody, unpredictable and potentially destructive youth.

The experience of fatherhood bewilders Stan. He looks back on his earlier days alone in the bush as a more positive experience. Family life leaves him without a real sense of possession — of having a centre or focus to his life.

In the family value-system presented by White, persons come together to assuage loneliness. They must overcome a silence that is within personal consciousness and a silence that is within external reality. But always the coming together, even for a life-long marriage, is more defensive than assertive. Consequently the family never acts as a confident mediative force. Internal changes tend to drive each person into defensive loneliness; external changes threaten the family's very existence.

Major disruptions centre upon Ray when he grows into early manhood. He becomes a ruthless opportunist and petty swindler. Knowing her son's predilections, Amy asks one day:

> "Do you think it was in him, anyway, all this badness? Or was it his upbringing? Or is it something that he has got from us? Together, I mean. It is like the cattle. Two goods can make a bad. We may not mix well," she said, and waited (p. 319).

Stan's response dramatizes his personal dilemma — his failure as a father or head of the household and his inability to find answers to the unanswerable questions haunting him:

> "I have never known what to do," he said, wincing. "I am to blame. I try to find the answers, but I have not succeeded yet. I do not understand myself or other people. That is all" (p. 319).

In White's presentation of a new-world family, long term living together does not penetrate another person's mystery. That remains inviolable. The only possible mediation is to accept another's mystery and to act in order to assuage another's pain:

> In time the man and woman came to accept each other's mystery . . . Habit comforted them, like warm drinks and slippers, and even went disguised as love (p. 342).

Thelma the daughter marries a lawyer and so enters the professional suburban middle class of a big city. The price she pays for her material success is to lose her sense of life's creative mystery. When this happens, in White's value-system, the person enters a sort of living death. Her suburban home, symbolising the quality of her family life, becomes "a fixed framework of light, round which tossed an unruly suggestion of trees that other people had planted" (p. 343). Her father, in contrast, achieves a flexible being — as he grows older, he "walked between the openings in the wind, his frank eyes watering a little from the sting" (p. 351).

The only relief to Stan's aloneness comes from his young grandson. Despite the fact that his father is Ray, a petty criminal, the boy possesses an insight into the mystery of things. He says one day to Stan:

> "Don't you ever know, Granpa, about things, because you just know?" (p. 407)

When Stan dies in old age, continuity of personal insight across the generations, despite the failure of one generation, is reinforced when his grandson dreams of writing "a poem of life, of all life, of what he did not know, but knew. Of all people, even the closed ones . . . " (p. 499).

For Patrick White, individual mystery remains impenetrable. No marriage, no nurturing of beloved partners and children, no neighbours, no community in the township of the bush or in the city suburbs can diminish for long this fundamental reality of personal separateness. Family life does not foster insight or individual growth. It is at best a force that acts negatively to protect its members.

Patrick White's presentation of a pioneering family shows the extreme limits of individualism. It is a powerful force for establishing a new society in frontier conditions, but it is weak in fashioning inter-generational family cohesiveness. Even the achievement of gaining insightful continuity across the generations is a mysterious, unpredictable and hence uncontrollable phenomenon. Its negative

reality does not foster new shared values but tends to reinforce separateness. Individuals are both the heroes and victims of the Australian family nexus; paradoxically the strengths of material compan-
ionship that the family offers may weaken personal insight, while an
individual's private journeying to deepen personal insight weakens
the family unit. In such a post-protestant, new-world culture as
White depicts, change itself becomes the dominant reality; and the
tyranny of change cannot be mediated by a strong family structure
—²only by a personal anguished search for permanent metaphysical
values.

(5)

V.S. Naipaul's *A House for Mr Biswas* (1961) portrays the
inter-generational experiences of an East Indian family in the racially-mixed Caribbean island of Trinidad. The time of events is
mainly the 1930s and 1940s when East Indians had achieved a distinctive lifestyle in the new society.

They had come as indentured labourers to the British West
Indies several generations earlier; although a few had returned to
India at the expiration of their contracts, the majority had stayed.
Of these, a small number had prospered, their extended family system forming the nucleus for business enterprise. These are represented in the novel by the socially formidable, all-powerful, ever-
watchful Tulsi clan.

Other East Indian immigrants had survived on the island,
eking a subsistence living from low-paid employment and handouts
from relatives; they often became dependent on the subtle patron-
age of more prosperous families such as the Tulsis; in *A House for Mr
Biswas* this process is ironically portrayed by Mr Biswas' absorption
into the Tulsi clan and his reluctant dependence upon it. But among
these energetic, luckless individuals who failed to demonstrate business acumen, there was often the dream of becoming a professional
person. The status of lawyer, doctor, dentist, journalist and teacher
was highly regarded. If many of Mr Biswas' generation, maturing in

the 1930s and 1940s could not reach this middleclass eminence, they dreamed their children would succeed in attaining the cherished heights.

Such a person is Mr Mohun Biswas. As Naipaul presents him, he represents a transitional generation; and for Mr Biswas the experience of transition — of being divided between languages, value systems, social classes, and ideals of personal success — is lifelong and painful.

This divisiveness, which characterizes also the family that adopts him and the family that he fathers, is evident from birth. Mohun Biswas was the son of a labourer but belonged to the Brahmin caste. Lacking the financial resources to enjoy the privileges of a Brahmin, he is dependent on the generosity of others. To enjoy the rights of his caste, he may live for a few hours away from the squalid mud hut which is his home and enter an affluent home dedicated to assisting needy Brahmins like himself. There the young boy could leave off his ragged clothes, wear a clean dhoti, savour good food, and accept the deferential service offered him. Naipaul points out that this early experience anticipates and symbolizes his whole future life:

> . . . he was respected as a Brahmin and pampered; yet as soon as the ceremony was over and he had taken his gift of money and cloth and left, he became once more only a labourer's child . . . And throughout his life his position was like that. As one of the Tulsi sons-in-law and as a journalist he found himself among people with money and sometimes with graces; with them his manner was unforcedly easy and he could summon up luxurious instincts; but always, at the end, he returned to his crowded, shabby room.[4]

The extended family system, structured upon Hindu concepts of responsibility, was itself becoming an anomaly in the restless, racially-mixed society of Trinidad. Religious values were diminishing, their public rituals assuming the emptiness of irrelevant repetition; the ancient language that enfolded and transmitted traditional values belonged to an ethnic minority in a society where English was the common tongue for East Indians, blacks, Chinese and the British administrative community; the knowledge revered by young Hindus was not Sanscrit spirituality but vocational training, professional expertise and ways to self-improvement in an entrepreneurial society.

The family profferring gifts and respect to the young Brahmin tried conscientiously to preserve religious values, rituals and commitments.

But very different are the Tulsis where, in contrast, traditional values have become seriously eroded. Mutual care is still extended to all relatives, but expediency rather than spiritual responsibility motivates the attention. Subordinating interpersonal relationships to making money and increasing family wealth is enshrined as the Tulsi collective goal.

As a young man Mohun Biswas married one of the Tulsi daughters — winning her not for his personal merits but because he was a Brahmin. Lacking money and training, he is unable to gain the status expected of a young married Hindu — become a householder. Instead his impoverished state makes him a *doolahin* — one, who lacking property, lives in his mother-in-law's household. Naipaul summarizes Mr Biswas' present circumstances and future attitude with the words:

> Mr Biswas had no money or position. He was expected to become a Tulsi.
> At once he rebelled (p.97).

As he reacts against family values and customs, his rebellion takes many forms. On a spiritual level he rejects the anodyne of Fate as the arbiter of human affairs. He determines to shape his own circumstances and not be passively dependent on Tulsis or others.

On an interpersonal level he rejects caste and sees opportunistic families like the Tulsis using both traditional Hindu customs and western business attitudes for private gain. He resents the hypocrisy involved in such a life posture. He personally tries to live a more honest life, exercising his talents in the expectation of modest rewards. In this he is influenced by the dominant values of the society surrounding him.

These stress individual effort, social reward and the benefits of belonging to a nuclear family. The values of the post-protestant work ethic have infiltrated the traditional East Indian family system, although some families still maintain appearances that suggest the contrary. Mr Biswas embraces these dominant individualist values and shuns the hypocrisy which disguises selfishness as altruism and family opportunism as spiritual benevolence.

But the realization of these individualist values is based on independence: Mohun Biswas must acquire an expertise, sell it for personal gain, acquire his own capital, and become a property owner in order to enjoy the status of belonging to a nuclear family in the style of the dominant culture. Untrained and ill-educated, he makes a gallant effort at attaining these goals. Although ultimately he fails, dying prematurely in his mid-forties, the man reveals his initiative, originality, talent and continual courage. The family he fathers shares his many tribulations and minor successes. Through his preferred values and social striving they have become a nuclear unit, free of the powerful Tulsi clan. Mohun Biswas attains the status of journalist, although is only a small figure in the island's newspaper circles. But he has opened a path along which his children will follow — away from forms of passive familial interdependence towards active assertive independence.

Naipaul's presentation of the conflicting value systems is barbed with multiple levels of irony. He sees Mr Biswas as a Chaplinesque failure rather than a work-ethic success; he notes that the status of householder remains as important in the western scale of values as in the Hindu one; Naipaul may respect personal ambition as a dynamic social force but he also perceives that it can reduce complex persons to isolated eccentrics. It may dessicate as well as energize.

Perhaps Naipaul is too deeply imbued — despite his rejection of other aspects of Hindu sprituality — with the view that there can be no creation without destruction, no pain without prior loss, no change of values or rituals without the period of transition that reduces whole generations to homelessness, exile and non-identity. Naipaul seems sadly to endorse the conclusion that neither the extended nor the nuclear family is able to mediate external change so as to endow positive benefits on its members. Always the force of change will sweep over human beings and the family is as prone to suffering and destruction as the isolated individual. Humanity has not yet devised an adequate protection against the power of change.

(6)

Summary

Family structure in all cultures is supported or enhanced by abstract values that in traditional societies derive from spiritual or religious systems. In new-world societies, the transference and transformation of values has generally weakened the structure of religions that were initially established in old-world societies. This, in turn, has served to weaken family structure. The new-world experience of living amid remote locations, frontier conditions and restless change has been an additional force in loosening traditional bonds of family cohesiveness.

Consequently, the family has been unable to satisfactorily mediate changes within its nexus; it has also had difficulty adjusting to psycho-social forces generated in the society at large.

Families, especially in new-world societies, have increasingly adopted negative postures towards the tyranny of restless change. The literary artist as radical analyst of his culture has revealed the constituents of the conflict and dramatized some of the defensive postures that have evolved. The general pattern that appears is a movement away from the mediative protection of religious and family organization. Thus individuals confront inescapable change alone. In this confrontation they may show courage or cowardice, assertiveness or submission, a will to associate with others or an acceptance of aloneness. Ironically their role, beneath the varieties of modern complex cultural formations, remains that of a pioneering adventurer preparing for whatever hazard the unknown terrain before him will present. But the unknown terrain is now the power of technology as for Euchariste Moisan in the United States' industrial system, subsistence living in the unknown but alluring city for Fabiano, Vitória and their children, suburbia or the criminal underworld for Stan and Amy Parker's children, and the enticements of entrepreneurial professionalism for Mr Biswas and his offspring.

1. Ringuet, *Trente arpents* (Montreal et Paris, 1967), p. 17.
2. Ramos, *Vidas Sêcas* (Lisboa, n.d.), p. 28.
3. White, *The Tree of Man* (London, 1956), pp. 63-4.
4. Naipaul, *A House for Mr Biswas* (London, 1969), p. 49.

Chapter Five

PROCESSES: SOCIO-POLITICAL STRUCTURE

A fella ain't got a soul of his
own, but only a piece of a big one.

John Steinbeck

(1)

The brevity of a new society's history reveals to a sensitive observer the arbitrariness of the values that have contributed to its making. From a wide variety of possible values available for importation or common to the indigenous population, some were chosen, adopted, implemented and institutionalized by the decisions of a ruling minority; others were ignored or discarded. For a radical analyst awareness of the culture's limited history and its arbitrary selection of values tends to provoke dissatisfaction with contemporary socio-political arrangements that have developed from the ruling elite's decisions; this awareness may be accompanied by the conviction that a finer organization of better values is both possible and desirable. The newness of new societies may thus arouse in sensitive minds the anguish of offended idealism. From this disillusionment come narratives analyzing the culture's socio-political experience.

Just as specific psycho-social values shape family structure, so specific socio-political experiences have shaped the consciousness of a society and its ruling elite. Radical analysis can uncover the values exercised by a controlling group and disseminated to the populace; it can show the effect of these prevailing assumptions upon the general population; and where there is a clash of conflicting interests, it can expose the developmental processes influencing the evolution of the whole culture. An artist as radical analyst tends to identify with the weaker group in any conflict of values and, from this perspective, may offer trenchant criticism of the values structuring the dominant groups.

A distinction may be drawn between two types of elite, each of which appears in different new-world countries: one is authoritarian and the other pragmatic.

A highly centralized authoritarian elite excludes as many people as possible from its decision-making, consolidates its power and privileges around as few persons as possible, and tends to reiterate continuously catch-phrases that encapsulate its value-system. Consequently, the structuring values tend to become immutable, their public symbols inviolable, and the society stagnant. Social and political revolution emerges as the only possiblity for effecting profound change.

Secondly, there is a pragmatic elite. This encourages participatory input of new ideas and solicits entry to its ranks from persons with a wide range of backgrounds, so as to convey appearances of sharing privileges and power; it tends to review continually the values and symbols which support its power and structure the whole society. It is usually eager for innovation, especially of a technological nature, provided all changes are channelled through its administrative services. It fosters orderly evolution and righteously bans revolution.

In exposing processes that, in his view, have shaped the society and its ruling group, an artist as radical analyst may dramatize either a single controlling figure or a collective phenomenon. Where there is the consciousness of authoritarianism, his presentation tends towards the former as in Miguel Ángel Asturias' *El Sēnor Presidente* and in many other South American novels showing the rule and effects of *caudillo* government; where there is the consciousness of a more open society, an artist as radical analyst tends to show the effects of the ruling elite's decision-making on type-figures representative of many persons in the society, such as Jennie in Ian Cross' *After Anzac Day*, the narrator in Rudy Wiebe's *The Scorched-Wood People* and Ma Joad in John Steinbeck's *The Grapes of Wrath*. His theme is not merely a malfunctioning socio-political process but the personal and collective suffering that follows from the failure to achieve a finer organization of values in the new society.

We shall look at these four narratives from different new-world societies; each exposes socio-political processes in order to analyse historical values and to imply the possibility of finer alternate ones.

(2)

One of the most terrifying presentations of the totalitarian leader and his dominance over a whole society is in Miguel Ángel Asturias' *El Señor Presidente*. Written during the 1930s, it was revised many times to meet Asturias' exacting linguistic refinements and was finally published in 1946. Deriving in part from personal experience of Guatemalan life during the presidency of Estrada Cabrera (1857-1924) who ruled the country with uncompromising ferocity from 1898 to 1920, the novel is a sombre prose-poem about the inhumanity that may arise in a culture dominated by an unchallengeable leader-figure. Estrada Cabrera conspired and killed to gain power; then, having been assisted by United States' financial and political interests in his struggle for supremacy, he was obliged after gaining power to grant them economic privileges; in return, they promised non-intervention in his national affairs while remaining a distantly supportive socio-political force.

Cabrera's dictatorship was ferocious and bloody; jails were crowded with political prisoners; the assassinations and secret executions of suspected dissidents were commonplace. A whole society lived in fear, the capital city becoming an echoing tomb of people afraid to converse in tones louder than whispers. Social and intellectual life stagnated under the rule of a watchful leader and his totalitarian elite.

Asturias' depiction of the man ruling over this cringing populace is remarkable for its psychological insights. His historical details are accurate; he shows the patriarch as having known poverty in childhood and, during adolescence, suffering real or imagined insults about his social background from richer youths; then, as a young unknown lawyer, without appropriate social contacts, he chose prostitutes, gamblers and horse-thieves as his clients. A dark disgust was generated in him at the struggle he had made to reach professional status; the disgust became resentment against the ruling elite of the rich and powerful; then the resentment became a smouldering suspicion-filled determination to make up for the long years when he had endured social and material deprivation.

Asturias shows that this ineradicable sense of deprivation, on which the man had brooded beyond the point of obsession, had motivated his single-minded rise to presidential power. Then, when he had gained supremacy, the same brooding suspicion compelled him to scrutinize the whole society for any signs of discontent or disloyalty. At the slightest hint, his embedded resentment became transformed into a vengeful, punitive force ordering arrests, imprisonment and executions. Although wielding total power, he could never convince himself of his absolute control. So, haunted by imaginary adversaries, he established a system in which informants, secret police and lowlife criminals terrorized the entire population. But he was still left with profound self-assurance of his right to rule.

Asturias' psychological poetry reveals the man's terrible contradictions. The socio-political omnipotence he had struggled for was never total; for his obsession with deprivation in turn deprived him of the satisfactions of power. He was pathetically prompted to continuing sequences of further repressions, further atrocities.

Several poetic images that take on surrealistic associations structure Asturias' presentation of the terrorized society and its stagnant culture.

One image is of the President's ears and is a finely conceived connotation linking this brooding figure with the political reality he has created. His ears augment both his private sexual gratifications and rumours about the public figures close to him in the social hierarchy. These rumours are brought to him by informants, for any person seeking personal advancement had to gain the President's ear; if suspected of disloyalty, gaining audience with the President was the only hope for clemency; if wishing to dispose of a rival or reinstate oneself in favour, whispering innuendoes about a fellow citizen was the surest way.

The Presidential Palace is surrounded by a small wood where guard dogs prowl. The trees are "made of ears" and, like the dogs' barks, form a network of threads which "connected every leaf to the President, keeping him informed of the townspeople's most secret thoughts."[1] Besides, the palace dogs have ears like door knockers (p.241); like the secret police they act in the President's interest. In a society where the citizens' most fearful experience is the knock of the secret police on the doors of their homes, the connection established between ears, watch-dogs, police and door knockers powerfully conveys the quality of life under the patriarch's governance.

A second structural image shows life in the abject society as a lottery where the Presidential will is stronger than Chance. He sees himself as the sole initiator of action — not Chance, or God. Because his whim, not principles of justice, determine a person's innocence or guilt, the image of the rigged lottery reveals the decay of objective values. As a citizen with defective speech asserts:

"Amigo, amigo, la única ley en egta tierra eg la lotería: pog lotería cae ugte en la cágcel, pog lotería lo fugilan, pog lotería lo hagen diputado, diplomático, pregidente de la Gepública, general, minigtro! De qué vale el egtudio aquí, si todo eg pog lotería?" (p.104)

"My friend, my friend, the only law on this earth is the lottery: the lottery can send you to prison, have you shot, make you a deputy, diplomat, President of the Republic, a general or a minister! What's the use of studying here if everything's determined by the lottery?"

The third structural image is of beggars. In such a sterile social system all inhabitants are effectively reduced to the level of beggars (Asturias' original idea was to write a story called "Los Mendugos políticos") and this condition of socio-politcal destitution is superbly captured in the novel's opening chapter.

It portrays the cathedral square of the capital city. The square is the home of the most indigent beggars. They haunt the night shadows of the magnificent cathedral; they sleep in the porch of El Señor — a name that connotes both christian deity and the secular presidential deity. They watch how soldiers and police make daily arrests, dragging their victims off to imprisonment or death. Unable or unwilling to relate to one another, these blind, deaf, lame, mentally deficient indigents evoke the prostratiop, helplessness and total sterility of a society rendered mal-functioning by its absolute leader.

Among them is an idiot who had never known a mother's consistent care. When anyone mocks him by calling aloud the word "Mother" he responds with anguished fury. His motherless condition also connotes the condition for the whole culture. The patriarch's monstrous paternalism has negated whatever modifying, softening and humanizing influences that an alternate, or female, presence might have offered. One of the consequences of a severely patriarchal culture is the destruction of the female principle; in its place comes ever more savage repression by the patriarch's soldiers, police, informants and sycophants: masculine values reign supreme to produce presidential and social impotence.

When, one evening, an unknown passerby mocks the idiot by calling the word "Mother", the young man leaps at him, mauling him to death. When the female principle is used only in mockery, the consequence is merciless aggression. The idiot's assault is only the first; worse is to come. The dead man was an army colonel and a close friend of the president. In response to one murder, the President unlooses a vaster terror upon the whole society.

So sharply etched are the details of human degradation and

so repressive is the socio-political atmosphere that Asturias establishes in the opening chapter which describes the beggars and the colonel's death that the even more atrocious subsequent events appear as inevitable and irremediable. In a society without norms, the most improbable happenings occur daily; in a culture where there are no openly shared responses to outrageous repressive incidents, the command of one man constitutes the only signal of communication. Surrealism becomes realism.

In effect, his power is god-like; and in the fourth structural image Asturias portrays the President as descendant of the Mayan god Tohil. In ancient Mayan myth and ritual, all creation depended upon Tohil's command. But to guarantee the return of the sun's light each day, Tohil required human sacrifices; and his subject worshippers willingly granted him his victims. So great was Tohil's need for appeasement by human sacrifices that the culture lost the distinction between norms of life and death. So there is neither true death nor true life in Asturias' poetic presentation of life under Presidential totalitarianism; with the President's assumption of god-like power and need for continual human sacrifices, death may be a release from persecution and life no more than an anguished death-like deprivation.

In *El Señor Presidente*, one of the first and greatest narratives exposing the effects of totalitarian rule over a new culture, Asturias shows omnipotence becoming impotence and cruelty appearing salvific. Suppression of the female principle, which would nurture moderating and humanizing influences, had produced a culture which, instead of fostering personal and collective fulfilment, only deepened personal and collective deprivation.

The most terrible deprivation is the destruction of hope and this, too, the President accomplishes. Asturias puts into the mouth of a governmental spokesman:

"... la regla de conducta del Señor Presidente es no dar esperanzas y pisotearlos y zurrarse en todos porque sí."(p.238)

". . . The President's rule of conduct is never to offer hope;
and people are crushed and beaten to death to make them
realize this."

A culture without hope encloses its members in a living death.
When sterilized by terror, a value-system can only wither. Asturias
saw no evolution for a culture reduced to the level of socio-political
indigence he experienced in the Guatemala of his youth and which
he dramatized in *El Señor Presidente*.

(3)

Unlike the closed totalitarian society concerned with reiter-
ating and promulgating loyalist god-like symbols, a more open society offers a radical analyst of its values fuller information on its ruling elite's processes of decision-making. Taking advantage of more
abundant data, the artist is free to dramatize those aspects of the
system that appear to him inadequate or malfunctioning. Where
idealism has been corroded by political practice, he can expose past
and present realities without running the risk of being murdered or
driven into exile for his revelations.

One of the most important novels evoking New Zealand's
socio-political experience is Ian Cross' *After Anzac Day* (1961). It
evokes approximately one hundred years of cultural heritage and
draws its contemporary drama from a national crisis which occurred during 1951.

The New Zealand dream that dazzled the minds of some
pioneering idealists was the establishment of an egalitarian society
in the South Pacific. If the worst excesses of class exploitation characterizing Britain and Europe generally were limited in the new
land by social legislation, it was thought that the two main islands
were able to accommodate a modest population capable of enjoying
adequate living standards. The dream took shape in the nineteenth
century; it was implemented by different governments in the twen-

tieth century but particularly by the Labour government of Michael Joseph Savage during the depression years of the late 1930s. Ian Cross shows some of the benefits accruing to the average working family from the innovative legislation of the time. He portrays Jennie, the daughter of a Maori mother and a white manual worker; she was a child when the Savage government introduced free milk and free dental care for schoolchildren. Later in life she remembers this and the first family allowances:

> She might have been made of gold when they started giving him money just because she was a child under sixteen; what a warm feeling it was for her, too, knowing that she was getting four shillings a week . . . There was free medicine, too.[2]

But New Zealand's entry into World War II placed restraints on developing the welfare state. During the war years, politicians had to put patriotism and armaments first; and military expenditure diverted funds from social services. Then, after 1945, when the Labour government might have been expected to implement further benefits, its strength declined. Cross comments on this phenomenon:

> . . . for the Labour Party never recovered from the war; the war cut the party adrift from its past, confused its doctrine. The soap-box orators from the streets of the 1920s were exhausted and there was no second generation to carry on: their social legislation had made it nearly impossible for them to perpetuate their own breed (p.151).

Opposition came from the country's traditional ruling elite. The large landowners and financiers had never abandoned their power and privileges. Despite reformers' dreams of an egalitarian society, their presence had remained constant and their political influence was ready to reassert itself openly. In the eyes of idealists and radicals, class divisiveness was disfiguring the new culture as surely as it had warped the old world that settlers had hopefully left behind. Now in 1951 a class conflict was about to break forth.

In one sequence Cross shows young Jennie looking out on the moonlit capital city of Wellington when a feeling of revulsion overcomes her:

> The decaying wood and corrugated iron looked like the shrivelled flesh of old men. Across this slop-basin of homes she saw the dark mass of pine trees on the side of the small hill, making a sort of sanitary towel behind which the Governor-General could have his great mansion and hold his garden parties (p.158).

Cross contrasts her and her working-class background with the long-established, socially secure Creighton family. In the mid-nineteenth century its founder had arrived in New Zealand with money to purchase property. He cleared the bush with his own hands, prospered and put his money into the purchase of more land. Although his son Henry rebelled against him at first, the boy was soon whipped back into patterns of conventional behaviour. A family dynasty was born. Henry married a parson's daughter, whose puritan values and emotional frigidity were replicated in their daughter, Margaret. She married John Rankin, a civil servant from a modest background, whose career flourished during the pre-1939 years of the Labour government. The implication is that the ruling class has retained its money, social status and privileges and also acquired a capacity to influence national policy through the Labour government. In effect it has joined with administrative power and given the illusion of being willing to help implement generous welfare legislation for the majority. But it can change loyalties when there are changes of power.

The novel's present action takes place in 1951. The Labour Party has been defeated in recent elections. A conservative government has taken over. Soon after it assumed power, the unions, supporters of the vanquished Labour Party, called a strike of waterfront workers. As a Minister of the new conservative government remarks:

> "No country in the world is quite so vulnerable to a water-front strike. Virtually all our national income is earned by primary produce carried by ships to the other side of the world."(p.174)

The strike becomes a trial of strength between a traditional ruling elite newly retured to power and protesting unions; the latter represent the less privileged majority, contain idealists of diverse persuasions, and are fearful of losing the benefits their members gained during the years of Labour government.

At this time of national crisis the conservative administration offers John Rankin a senior position where he will work to break the strike. He is a man of humble origins who has furthered his career by making effective compromises and a strategic, if unhappy, marriage. His training as a civil servant overcomes early class loyalties and he accepts the key post offered him. In an evolutionary culture, a pragmatic elite is able to co-opt talented individuals from outside its ranks to work against larger power groups representing workers, unions and the Labour Party.

Despite affluence and apparent victories — the strike is broken — Ian Cross' presentation of the Creighton-Rankin family emphasizes the quality of loss. The family's and ruling elite's power are at their height; but he stresses that, inwardly, they are a passionless family, vitiated by several generations of life-denying puritanism; they lack the emotional depth and experience that characterized the family's founder, so the later generations do not fully understand the severity of the constraints their administrative decisions are imposing on the whole society. His implication is: can persons with such inauthentic personal relationships effectively determine the fate of an entire society? In Ian Cross' ironic vision of New

Zealand culture, such families have taken greatly from the society's resources to build their own fortunes and ambitions; they have given back little, either to the land or the people. He shows them a grotesque family — benign but short-sighted, seeming to be concerned with the majority's welfare but, in fact, emotionally immature and self-centered. They are a model of right-wing pseudo-benevolence in an evolving social democracy.

In contrast, Jennie and her racially-mixed working-class family possess more genuine values. Unlike the Creighton-Rankins, their family fortunes have declined over the years. But during the time of national discord, Jennie is pregnant and, in the symbolism of the novel, the coming child might suggest a more fruitful alliance between the classes for the future shaping of New Zealand society. For John Rankin, about to take on further administrative power, cares greatly for the child and the mother. Cross suggests that the spiritual destitution of the Creighton-Rankin family and, by implication of the monied, landowning-administrative elite, may be relieved, if human fellow-feeling replaces self-centeredness and bland indifference to others. Cross sees that these attitudes, which result from a puritan value-system, treat the mass of people as mere manipulable bureaucratic units; they must be transformed into a compassionate concern for all citizens, if New Zealand culture is to fulfil its former dreams. For unlike Guatemala and other South American societies, New Zealand was born in hope. By continuing to draw upon its abundant reserves of hope, its cultural evolution can be steadily maintained.

(4)

The problems of absorbing ethnic minorities into a developing new culture are many and complex. Only belatedly has come an awareness that their survival within a total nexus of multiculturalism is possible or desirable. Too often the past assumption has been that the political allegiance of minority groups to the central government depended on their abandoning distinctive cultural traits and becoming absorbed into the dominant developing value-system. In the Dominion of Canada this had provoked a long resentment among the people of Quebec and in other Francophone communities scattered across country.

Two of Canada's major developmental crises in the nineteenth century centered on the Metis — their rebellion at Red River in 1869 and at Batoche in 1885. Their protests against the treatment accorded them by the federal government were the strongest resistance to a determined Canadian expansionism organized by men intent on constructing a nation that stretched from the Atlantic to the Pacific.

The Metis roamed over and derived a living from large tracts of central territory. They blocked national expansion.

They were free spirits. Intermarriage from the early seventeenth century between French trappers and native Indians had produced a rugged individualist termperament softened only by the deepest loyalties to fellow Metis, one's personal family, and the Catholic parish to which they belonged. The Metis had spread far across the West, taken possession of some choice lands and they rightly sensed, by the early nineteenth century, that they were a "nation" — that is, possessors of a unique and viable culture that merited recognition by government administrators.

But suppression rather than recognition was their political destiny. Legal title to the territory on which they lived was held by the Anglophone Hudson's Bay Company which sold it to the federal government to help realize the dream of confederation. This came about in 1867. But there was no consultation over land rights with the Metis who feared that their culture, property claims and means of livelihood were imperilled. In 1869 they made their first revolt by preventing the bearer of the new federal authority from entering their territory. They declared their territorial autonomy, and hostilities grew; but eventually compromises were agreed upon and the Province of Manitoba was established. Specific rights were guaranteed to the Meti minority in the new province, but these rights were to be steadily eroded by political manoeuverings over the next generations.

Rudy Wiebe's *The Scorched-Wood People* (1977) — the title translates the phrase descriptive of the Metis, *les bois brûlés* — dramatizes in the first of its narrative sequences the armed rebellion at Red River in 1869 and its aftermath. In exposing the details of this developmental process, the consequences of which were to reverberate throughout Canadian evolution, Wiebe remains insistently sympathetic to the Metis. An unnamed Meti narrator nostalgically looks back on these events and evokes the past grandeur of his "nation". Part of that grandeur was embodied in the leaders of the time — Gabriel Dumont and Louis Riel. In some respects they were the finest flowers of their culture. The presentation Wiebe offers of the natural military genius Gabriel Dumont is similar to Euclides da Cunha's presentation of Antônio Conselheiro: each author makes the physical features of the two men akin to the land where they were born and grew. Their characters and consciousness are formed from the physical space and geographical realities of their particular new-world environments: Dumont's face is

> like a cliff undercut by a prairie river from one year to the next; he and his brothers and their people were their own lords, their only rulers the sky and the long land and slow muddy loops of prairie rivers, and the buffalo, their true kind and ruler who gave them everything for life and happiness.[3]

But expansionism from Eastern Canada threatened these geographical and spriritual freedoms. In Wiebe's dramatization, the Metis anticipated the influx of immigrants, many of whom were likely to be non-Francophones; they feared a new language would replace French; land holdings would be reapportioned — already surveyors have trespassed on Meti property; excess killing of buffalo would threaten their food supply; a new legal system would replace traditional community law; and, not least, different religious values would motivate the Anglo-Scots' federal administrators from the French-Catholic values structuring Meti belief and behaviour.

Wiebe, like Euclides da Cunha, remains close to documentary details of the actual historical struggle in constructing his narrative. To dramatize the conflicting values he characterizes two men, each a leader for his side and each a real-life personage.

One the one hand there is the Federal Government's Special Commissioner Donald Smith — a self-denying, puritanically disciplined Scotsman, whose personal prudence becomes political shrewdness when manipulating fellow Anglo-Scots to his viewpoints and policies.

On the other side stands Gabriel Dumont — boisterous in his pleasures, always conscious of family and community loyalties, committed to Meti Catholicism, illiterate and uneducated, but accurately intuitive in his perceptions and policies.

In Donald Smith a cold administrative rationality intent on a prepared course of action was confronting Dumont's poetically instinctive heart and head. There is an inevitability about the defeat of Dumont, representative of his people and their traditions. Wiebe's narrator is frequently ironic about the emergent new Anglophone culture that was consciously spreading westward, confronting the old Francophone values and, in the process, destroying them. He sees the federal politicians "forging" (there is a deliberate ambiguity in the choice of verb) a new nation "out of a small complex of confronting hatreds rebalanced at every election with infinite care" (p.88). In their manipulations the federal politicians, together with their administrators, turned their backs on the possibility of a bicultural compromise; this would have protected Meti valuĕs and enabled them to participate as a minority group in the totality of the new culture, rather than be submerged by it. In actual Canadian experience almost another hundred years were to elapse before that possibility reappeared as a desirable national objective.

In the expansionist Anglophone mood of the mid-nineteenth century, Ontarian "nationalism" was a prime motivating power. The Meti submission to federal authority after the collapse of their short-lived rebellion of 1869 strengthened this Eastern expansionism and hastened the consolidation of the nation-state. Although the federal government had promised to protect Francophone culture in the new province of Manitoba, many promises were soon abandoned or conveniently forgotten by the newly established provincial government. The Metis and their leaders became either actual, or symbolic, exiles from their traditional ways of life.

Sixteen years later in the more westerly territory of Saskatchewan a similar conflict repeated itself. It grew to become a more direct confrontation between Metis and the federal Government, with the contrasting values more nakedly polarized. The federal government, still determined to complete its East-West linkage for the new nation-state, pressed on with construction of the national railway. By this time the Metis were severely demoralized; and because of diminishing buffalo herds they were struggling against annual starvation. Over the intervening years, Louis Riel, the second dominant figure in the Red River rebellion, having been denied his place as a parliamentary spokesman for his people, had grown embittered and somewhat deranged in the loneliness of exile within the United States. But when called to assist his people in a last struggle against further encroachments on their lands and culture, he returned and showed great skill at rapidly infusing new hope to a bewildered and humiliated group. The second narrative sequence of *The Scorched-Wood People* dramatizes his power in the events leading to the final confrontation between Metis and federal military might at Batoche, Saskatchewan, in 1885.

To restore dignity to his broken "nation" he had to discard the authority of Catholicism — a seemingly impossible task among a populace with primitive but deeply imbued beliefs. But for a time he succeeded in swaying them by the revelations he offered of his own prophetic visions. Approximately nine hundred followers accepted

him; and he led them, ironically, into a form of primitive protestantism while retaining the rituals of traditional catholicism. He taught
them to determine:

> whether they personally had the confidence in themselves
> to decide they would believe something they had not been
> taught always to believe, that a personal decision about faith
> not dictated by a priest but directly and personally commu-
> nicated by God was even possible, and that a priest could
> then only corroborate or, if he refused to do that, he was
> damnably *wrong* (p.283).

In effect, Riel's "revelations" offered a new structure of being; he
was able, in the shortest time, to modify a traditional belief-system
and establish a new legitimate authority from which to energize political struggle. The achievement was distinctively his alone. Its out-
come for his Meti followers was a sudden growth in personal and
collective self-esteem. Wiebe's narrator retrospectively comments:

> To see our people ride like that: excitement, pride, brother-
> hood, and ceremony all together are not easily found on
> earth, especially by the poor; they must be enjoyed for that
> fleeting moment in which they touch us, for pain and per-
> haps agony are then never far away (p.261).

But it was a short-lived exhilaration. Despite Dumont's superb strategies, the rebel group's military resistance was soon destroyed; Riel
was executed, Dumont driven into exile; and Meti submission to
federal authority was harshly reinforced.

Wiebe exposes the details of the most heroic dramatic incidents in Canadian westward expansion; in doing so he reveals the
clash between the values of the ruling Eastern Canadian elite and
those of a once-proud indigenous population. In retrospect, the minority group was doomed to defeat. The political, financial and

military forces against them were too great. And despite Riel's magnificent invention of an energizing myth to rally his followers, the myth of making a new nation from Atlantic to Pacific, sedulously promulgated by the Eastern ruling elite, was more potent and pervasive.

In exposing these processes contributing to Canadian cultural growth, Wiebe shows the bewilderment that follows external assaults upon a minority community's behavioral pattern. The bewilderment leads the group to question its basic life values. A loss of self-esteem results. Only prolonged self-abasement can follow. The process is familiar to colonized groups, classes and nations the world over. The problem in the making or reorganizing of any society is how to restore positive values so that collective dignity may be reborn. It was Riel's wondrous achievement to accomplish this for a brief period.

The Scorched-Wood People implicitly attacks the comfortable Canadian belief that Canadian identity evolves slowly from a mosaic of sub-cultures; each of which, it is assumed, freely exists for as long as it chooses, contributing to the cultural enrichment of the whole. The federal authority's treatment of Meti culture, in history and in Wiebe's dramatization, offers little to verify the myth of ethnic cultural autonomy. But by exposing the developmental crises at Red River in 1869 and Batoche in 1885, Wiebe reasserts the proposition that all cultures have values worthy of preservation. Only after dominant governing elites recognize this can a genuine multicultural mosaic be attained. The Canadian myth becomes real when an active multiculturalism beckons as a desirable distant objective.

(5)

Socio-political forces stand in opposition to family values in John Steinbeck's *The Grapes of Wrath* (1939). The Joad family represents a value-system, life-attitude and pioneering class that contributed mightily to the making of United States' culture. But in the

1930s, when the country suffered its severest economic depression, the individualist and collectivist values of such groups were eroded; their life-style was threatened and, as in the case of the Canadian Metis, their sense of dignity imperilled.

Farming families like the Joads were unprotected by governmental tariffs and marketing boards; they were dependent for a livelihood upon successful retailing of their annual crops; if the crops failed or the market yielded only low prices, they were unable to meet mortgage payments on land or farming equipment. External economic forces could deprive them of their property; and when families like the Joads lost their land, the only way of life they knew was destroyed. They were lost and bewildered people. Like their forebears, they became migrants. Their ancestors had crossed the seas to come to the United States; in the 1930s the Joad family, and the millions they represent, crossed the United States to find new hope in a new state. The Joads headed from Oklahoma to the western state of California.

But California was controlled by an elite more sophisticated than any these internal migrants had previously encountered. It was a new organization of power so concentrated in its holdings and so oblique in the diffusion of its strength that ascribing responsibility for its malfunctioning was difficult or impossible. But obviously maladministration of large proportions was responsible for the suffering imposed on millions of people Before writing *The Grapes of Wrath*, Steinbeck used his skills as an investigative journalist to examine the new California system. He exposed its working in a pamplet called *Their Blood is Strong* published in 1938.

In his view California had established a system of interlocking capital. The interests of the ruling elite had combined to control large tracts of farming land, distributive facilities, banks, news media, public utilities and — where necessary — local politicians. The effect on farming was decisive. The new organization of agribusiness was comparable to feudal overlordship, with the difference that there was difficulty discerning who was the overlord. But the power of the controllers was absolute:

> The large farms in California are organized as closely and
> are as centrally directed in their policy as are the industries
> and shipping, the banking and public utilities.[4]

But to Steinbeck's eyes the system remains alertly suspi-
cious. Shrewdly he sees current Californian conditions as a model
for totalitarianism:

> It would almost seem that having built the repressive atti-
> tude toward the labor they need to survive, the directors
> were terrified of the things they have created. This fear dic-
> tates an increase of the repressive method, of greater num-
> ber of guards, and a constant suggestion that the ranch is
> armed to fight.[5]

Unlike the Guatemala of Estrada Cabrera and Asturias' vision, California — and by implication the United States — has not yet made
the repression total. The coercive apparatus exists, but has not yet
been fully implemented. Within the interstices of freedom still al-
lowed the workless and impoverished, the new-world restlessness
can still function. But to what purpose?

Steinbeck imagines the victimized organizing to form
a countervailing power to that of the socio-political elite. His vision
is poetic. It is put into the life experience and words of Preacher
Jim Casy.

A travelling clergyman with a sullied reputation, he em-
bodies the spirit of new-world freedom. Journeying with the Joads
and other families, he becomes more convinced that the life-force in
people is being destroyed; what is best in them is being over-
whelmed by social repression and economic mismanagement. To
pray seems a useless exercise:

"Listen to people a-talkin', an' purty soon I hear the way

folks are feelin' . . . When they'd get so hungry they couldn' stan' it no more, why, they'd ast me to pray for 'em, an' sometimes I done it . . . Use ta rip off a prayer an' all the troubles'd stick to that prayer like flies on flypaper, an' the prayer'd go a-sailin' off, a'takin' them troubles along. But it don't work no more."[6]

But Casy senses that out of the innate restlessness of the people a new force is being born. It is a form of group solidarity. He sees that people robbed of their human dignity may abandon traditional notions of individual achievement and individual salvation. In place of individualism comes a sense that all the poor are indivisible: each person "ain't got a soul of his own, but only a piece of a big one"(p.463); so the struggle must be to give social realization to this oneness. When this is accomplished, a countervailing power will be born and then it will stand in opposition to the power of the ruling elite.

In the meantime families must hold together, for group solidarity will be achieved by family unionization. The burden for this lies with the women. Only female strength can offer positive immediate values to the suffering; only female strength can achieve continuity between the members of the family when economic forces encourage dislocation, despondency and destruction. Upon the basis of female supportiveness, magnificently symbolized by Ma Joad, a new social justice will appear and a lost dignity will return to the victimized.

Steinbeck's distress at a lost freedom and a betrayed sociopolitical ideal pervades *The Grapes of Wrath*. His criticism of depression conditions is minor compared with his radical analysis of the hidden totalitarianism already developed in his native state of California. The United States' economic evolution had produced the developmental crisis of the decade-long depression of the 1930s; but the larger developmental crisis, to his contemporary view, lay in the consequences of the corporate vertical and horizontal integration which entrenched a form of totalitarianism. By 1939 Steinbeck's radical analysis had exposed the origins of United States' agribusiness and conglomerate capitalism. He wrote *The Grapes of Wrath* as a warning and a forecast of the greater power that was to consolidate itself and expand internationally in the years ahead.

(6)

Summary

New-world societies demonstrate a variety of governmental forms possessing different degrees of legitimacy. The treatment that the ruling elite accords the populace varies historically as much as geographically; but the lives of the majority are always dependent on the values exercised by the controlling group.

The radical analysis of the diverse forms of authoritarianism made by literary artists as different as Asturias, Wiebe and Steinbeck identifies absolute control as a corrosive male force: it exists and perpetuates itself by denying a female principle that may modify absoluteness, soften rigidified relationships and humanize society. Prolonged denial of humane values whether by El Señor Presidente, the nineteenth-century expansionist Canadian government concerned with overcoming a racial obstacle, or United States' conglomerate capitalism leads to the organization of opposition; the writers show that where there is no compromise between ruling elite and its opposition only repression, rebellion and a terrorized defeatist society can result.

More evolutionary processes show a capacity to absorb divergent ideals, attitudes and persons; they can incorporate them partially or wholly into the dominant culture's development. Although crises may occur, such as the New Zealand waterfront strike of 1951 portrayed by Ian Cross, pragmatic values offer both continuity and hope. They hold the possibility of admitting minority groups, recognizing them as sub-cultures, and perceiving the desirability, as a socio-political goal, of multiculturalism in the new society.

1. Asturias, *El Señor Presidente* (Buenos Aires, 1964), p.40.
2. Cross, *After Anzac Day* (London, 1961), pp.11-12.
3. Wiebe, *The Scorched-Wood People* (Toronto, 1977), p.11.
4. French, *A Companion to The Grapes of Wrath* (New York, 1963) p.65.
5. French, p.68.
6. Steinbeck, *The Grapes of Wrath* (New York, 1978), p.275.

Chapter Six

RADICAL ANALYSIS OF CULTURAL FORMATION

A New World, a New Dimension of Being.

Scott Symons

An artist in a new-world culture functions in a different intellectual and emotional context from his counterpart in the world's older cultures. A spirit of restlessness, characteristic of the new culture itself, fosters a radical analysis that induces him to scrutinize both cultural origins and the processes that have made the functioning value-system.

Cultural growth is a continuous phenomenon, but major developments tend to pivot upon distinctive clashes of values. The resultant conflicts expose forms of necessity to which new responses must be made. Some former historical responses offered inadequate solutions, others temporary solutions, and many demanded further analysis at a later date.

Many new-world artists undertake this analysis with vigour and commitment. They examine formative influences, dramatize changes in psycho-social and socio-political relationships, offer alternate values to those that emerged from former developmental crises, and engage with the cultural processes in freshly imaginative and innovative ways. Because their culture is less fixed in mannered traditions and intellectual styles than older societies, their imaginative presentations can be made in the hopeful idealism of improving conditions for fellow-members of the society.

Offering alternate values may meet with varied responses from persons of influence and the general public; these may range from the destructive to the sycophantic or the indifferent.

An unhealthy culture tends to disregard innovation; it may act to suppress or segregate alternate values arising from artists, intellectuals or populace; its triumphant but sterile institutions of government, finance, law and religion will seek to outlaw innovation and punish the innovator; this is the sad fate of artists, intellectuals and popular leaders in many South American countries.

The weakness of this response, in our present emerging globalism, is that it must become increasingly authoritarian in order to prevent alternate values appearing and being disseminated. In an age of immediate communications, new ideas are the life-force of culture and consciousness. To deny them is to deny life itself. In the emergent era of globalism, denial is only deferral.

A healthy culture, on the other hand, aware that continual change is currently inescapable, acknowledges the necessity of alternate values and assumes that they cannot exist in a vacuum without causing damage to the social fabric. So they are integrated into the value-system. A healthy culture is insistently concerned with making, unmaking and remaking values in a process of continual self-adjustment. It accepts the infiltration of new ideas to modify, re-form and transvalue existing social relationships.

The strength of this response lies in its general objective. This may be outlined as giving richer dimensions to human experience and producing for its members, both personally and collectively, a deeper sense of relationship to society and cosmos. When alternate values diverge from commonly accepted ideals, the system may seek to restrain but not suppress them. A healthy culture accepts new ideas and alternate values as the life-force of consciousness.

In effect, whether its historical origins are ancient or recent, a healthy culture experiences the restlessness characteristic of new societies. The triumph of contemporary communications is the triumph of restlessness. No ideal based on the static or unchanging aspects of assumed Truth can survive. The extirpation of new ideas, values or attitudes by the banning of books, control of the media and the execution of heretics can only condemn the extirpator to desolating insularity and sterilizing self-condemnation. Ages, soci-

eties and institutions characterizing themselves by the fixed establishment of Eternal Truth have crumbled before the age of Invention, innovation and pragmatic modification. The triumph of new
cultures is precisely that they had prior experience of the attitudes
characterizing the new age before the new age was born. Almost all
cultures in the world today experience the clash of values, the struggle for unique self-articulation and the need to constantly develop
new modes of perception. But these phenomena have been central
to the emergence of new societies in North and South America, the
Caribbean and the South Pacific. They are, in a sense, the oldest
societies in the new global reality.

Some have been more successful than others. The most
richly experienced of them have succeeded in transforming the basic necessity of frontier and pioneering conditions into individual
needs; relieved of the struggle for survival, the person can then
choose between variables without encountering the agony of brute
necessity. A later stage of evolution changed personal needs into
preferences: these can be superficially satisfied by consumer services but the freedom gained by the cultural evolution also offered
free time for individual probings into the spiritual mysteries encompassing all life.

Less successful new societies have left the mass of their population living in conditions of basic necessity. The frontier has disap-
peared and a large economy has been built to support the nation-
state; but, by various stratagems through decades or centuries, the
ruling elites have limited the choices available to the mass and kept
them in a survival posture.

In each type of society the articulations of the serious artist
are essential. By acting as a radical analyst of his culture and exposing its formation, he can open blocked perspectives and offer hope.
The work of William Carlos William in the United States, Pablo Neruda in Chile, Edward Brathwaite and Aimé Césaire in the Caribbean, Patrick White in Australia reveals the vision and integrity necessary for such a role. New-world restlessness and radical analysis of

cultural formation have become harnessed to produce new insights into human relationships; and, further, new insights into humanity's relationships with necessity, needs and preferences.

The conscious process of making a culture is unique in human experience. Perhaps, in the past, only the strategies for expanding institutionalized religions — in particular christianity and islam — have been comparable. But in the present age of emergent globalism, when all cultures are being drawn into a convergent web, the process of making and re-making cultures becomes the general human experience.

Older societies must accept alternate values to renew their traditional values; if they fail to do so, modern communications will impose on them the perspective of the dominant cultures. In seeking to renew, such societies must look at new-world cultures where the largest experiments in planned human migration, organized land settlement, racial inter-relationship and technological innovation have taken place. From these experiences, planners may derive elements that will assist the pragmatic reordering of older societies. And hovering daily nearer for all societies is the time of the cultural engineer; he will be responsibile for inaugurating empirical structured responses to the new necessity of global integration. Never has the challenge been greater for humanity to shape new goals, define new freedoms and glory in new insights.

SELECTED BIBLIOGRAPHY

Asturias, Miguel Ángel, *El Señor Presidente* (Editorial Losada, S.A. Buenos Aires) 1964, 4th ed.

Brathwaite, Edward, *The Arrivants: A New World Trilogy* (Oxford University Press, London) 1977.

Carpentier, Alejo, *Los pasos perdidos* (Compañia general de ediciones, S.A. Mexico) 1966, 2nd ed.

Cross, Ian, *After Anzac Day* (Andre Deutsch, London) 1961.

Cunha, Euclides da, *Os Sertões* (Livraria Francisco Alves, Rio de Janeiro) 1968, new ed.

Echeverría, Roberto Gonzales, *Alejo Carpentier: The Pilgrim at Home* (Cornell University Press, Ithaca) 1977.

Faulkner, William, *The Unvanquished* (Random House, New York) 1965.

García Márquez, Gabriel, *El otoño del patriarca* (Plaza y Janés, Barcelona) 1975.

Giacomin, Helmy F. (ed.) *Homenajae a Alejo Carpentier* (Las Americas Publishing Co. New York) 1970.

Giguère, Roland, *L'age de la parole, poèmes 1949-1960* (Editions de l'hexagone, Ottawa) 1965.

Gutteridge, Don, *A True History of Lambton County* (Oberon, Ottawa), 1977.

Hemingway, Ernest, *The Short Stories* (Scribners, New York) 1938.

Laurence, Margaret, *The Diviners* (Knopf, New York) 1957.

Miron, Gaston, *L'homme rapaillé* (Les Presses de l'Université de Montréal, Montréal) 1970.

Naipaul, V.S. *A House for Mr Biswas* (Penguin Books, England) 1969.

Neruda, Pablo, *Obras completas* (Editorial Losada, Buenos Aires) 1962, 2nd ed. aumentada.

Newlove, John, *Black Night Window* (McClelland & Stewart, Toronto) 1968.

O'Hagan, Howard, *The Woman Who Got on at Jasper Station and Other Stories* (Alan Swallow, Denver) 1963.

Préfontaine, Yves, *Pays sans parole* (Editions de l'hexagone, Ottawa) 1967.

Ramos, Graciliano, *Vidas Sêcas* (Portugalia Editora, Lisbon) n.d.

Ringuet, *Trente arpents* (Fides, Montréal et Paris) 1967.

Rosa, João Guimarães, *Grande Sertão: Veredas* (José Olympio, Rio de Janeiro) 8th ed.

Sargeson, Frank, *Collected Stories 1935-1963* (Blackwood & Janet Paul, Auckland) 1964.

Steinbeck, John, *The Grapes of Wrath* (Viking Press, New York) 1978 rep.

White, Landeg, *V.S. Naipaul: A Critical Introduction* (Macmillan, London) 1975.

White, Patrick, *The Tree of Man* (Eyre & Spottiswoode, London) 1956.

White, Patrick, *Voss* (Viking Press, New York) 1957.

Wiebe, Rudy, *The Scorched-Wood People* (McClelland & Stewart, Toronto) 1977.

Williams, William Carlos, *Paterson* (New Directions, New York) 1948.

COSTERUS.

Volume 1. Amsterdam 1972. 240 p. Hfl. 40.—
GARLAND CANNON: Sir William Jones's Translation-Interpretation of San-skrit Literature. SARAH DYCK: The Presence of that Shape: Shelley's *Prometheus Unbound.* MARJORIE ELDER: Hawthorne's *The Marble Faun:* A Gothic Structure. JAMES L. GOLDEN: Adam Smith as a Rhetorical Theorist and Literary Critic. JACK GOODSTEIN: Poetry, Religion and Fact: Matthew Arnold. JAY L. HALIO: Anxiety in *Othello.* JOHN ILLO: Miracle in Milton's Early Verse. F. SAMUEL JANZOW: De Quincey's "Danish Origin of the Lake Country Dialect" Republished. MARTIN L. KORNBLUTH: The Degeneration of Classical Friendship in Elizabethan Drama. VIRGINIA MOSELY: The "Dangerous" Paradox in Joyce's "Eveline". JOHN NIST: Linguistics and the Esthetics of English. SCOTT B. RICE: Smollett's *Travels* and the Genre of Grand Tour Literature. LISBETH J. SACHS and BERNARD H. STERN: The Little Preoedipal Boy in Papa Hemingway and How He Created His Artistry.

Volume 2. Amsterdam 1972. 236 p. Hfl. 40.—
RALPH BEHRENS: Mérimée, Hemingway, and the Bulls. JEANNINE BOHL-MEYER: Mythology in Sackville's "Induction" and "Complaint". HAROLD A. BRACK: Needed — a new language for communicating religion. LEONARD FEINBERG: Satire and Humor: In the Orient and in the West. B. GRANGER: The Whim-Whamsical Bachelors in Salmagundi. W. M. FORCE: The What Story? or Who's Who at the Zoo? W. N. KNIGHT: To Enter lists with God. Transformation of Spencerian Chivalric Tradition in Paradise Regained. MARY D. KRAMER: The Roman Catholic Cleric on the Jacobean Stage. BURTON R. POLLIN: The Temperance Movement and Its Friends Look at Poe. SAMUEL J. ROGAL: Two Translations of the Iliad, Book I: Pope and Tickell. J. L. STYAN: The Delicate Balance: Audience Ambivalence in the Comedy of Shakespeare and Chekhov. CLAUDE W. SUMERLIN: Christopher Smart's A Song to David: its influence on Robert Browning. B.W. TEDFORD: A Recipe for Satire and Civilization. H. H. WATTS: Othello and the Issue of Multiplicity. GUY R. WOODALL: Nationalism in the Philadelphia National Gazette and Literary Register: 1820—1836.

Volume 3. Amsterdam 1972. 236 p. Hfl. 40.—
RAYMOND BENOIT: In Dear Detail by Ideal Light: "Ode on a Grecian Urn". E. F. CALLAHAN: Lyric Origins of the Unity of 1 Henry IV. FRASER DREW: John Masefield and Juan Manuel de Rosas. LAURENCE GONZALEZ: Persona Bob: seer and fool. A. HIRT: A Question of Excess: Neo-Classical Adaptations of Greek Tragedy. EDWIN HONIG: Examples of

Poetic Diction in Ben Jonson. ELSIE LEACH: T. S. Eliot and the School of Donne. SEYMOUR REITER: The Structure of 'Waiting for Godot'. DANIEL E. VAN TASSEL: The Search for Manhood in D. H. Lawrence's 'Sons and Lovers'. MARVIN ROSENBERG: Poetry of the Theatre. GUY R. WOODALL: James Russell Lowell's "Works of Jeremy Taylor, D.D.'

Volume 4. Amsterdam 1972. 233 p. Hfl. 40.–
BOGDDY ARIAS: Sailor's Reveries. R. H. BOWERS: Marlowe's 'Dr. Faustus', Tirso's 'El Condenado por Desconfiado', and the Secret Cause. HOWARD O. BROGAN: Satirist Burns and Lord Byron. WELLER EMBLER: Simone Weil and T. S. Eliot. E. ANTHONY JAMES: Defoe's Autobiographical Apologia: Rhetorical Slanting in 'An Appeal to Honour and Justice'. MARY D. KRAMER: The American Wild West Show and "Buffalo Bill" Cody. IRVING MASSEY: Shelley's "Dirge for the Year": The Relation of the Holograph to the First Edition. L. J. MORRISSEY: English Street Theatre: 1655–1708. M. PATRICK: Browning's Dramatic Techniques and 'The Ring and the Book': A Study in Mechanic and Organic Unity. VINCENT F. PETRONELLA: Shakespeare's 'Henry V' and the Second Tetralogy: Meditation as Drama. NASEEB SHAHEEN: Deriving Adjectives from Nouns. TED R. SPIVEY: The Apocalyptic Symbolism of W. B. Yeats and T. S. Eliot. EDWARD STONE: The Other Sermon in 'Moby–Dick'. M. G. WILLIAMS: 'In Memoriam': A Broad Church Poem.

Volume 5. Amsterdam 1972. 236 p. Hfl. 40.–
PETER G. BEIDLER: Chaucer's Merchant and the Tale of January. ROBERT A. BRYAN: Poets, Poetry, and Mercury in Spenser's Prosopopia: Mother Hubberd's Tale. EDWARD M. HOLMES: Requiem For A Scarlet Nun. E. ANTHONY JAMES: Defoe's Narrative Artistry: Naming and Describing in Robinson Crusoe. MICHAEL J. KELLY: Coleridge's "Picture, or The Lover's Resolution": its Relationship to "Dejection" and its Sources in the Notebooks. EDWARD MARGOLIES: The Playwright and his Critics. MURRAY F. MARKLAND: The Task Set by Valor. RAYMOND S. NELSON: Back to Methuselah: Shaw's Modern Bible. THOMAS W. ROSS: Maimed Rites in Much Ado About Nothing. WILLIAM B. TOOLE: The Metaphor of Alchemy in Julius Caesar. PAUL WEST: Carlyle's Bravura Prophetics. GLENA D. WOOD: The Tragi-Comic Dimensions of Lear's Fool. H. ALAN WYCHERLEY: "Americana": The Mencken – Lorimer Feud.

Volume 6. Amsterdam 1972. 235 p. Hfl. 40.–
GEORG W. BOSWELL: Superstition and Belief in Faulkner. ALBERT COOK: Blake's Milton. MARSHA KINDER: The Improved Author's Farce: An Analysis of the 1734 Revisions. ABE LAUFE: What Makes Drama Run? (Introduction to Anatomy of a Hit). RICHARD L. LOUGHLIN: Laugh and Grow Wise with Oliver Goldsmith. EDWARD MARGOLIES: The American Detective Thriller & The Idea of Society. RAYMOND S. NELSON: Shaw's Heaven, Hell, and Redemption. HAROLD OREL: Is Patrick White's Voss the Real Leichhardt of Australia? LOUIS B. SALOMON: A Walk With Emerson On The Dark Side. H. GRANT SAMPSON: Structure in the Poetry of Thoreau. JAMES H. SIMS, Some Biblical Light on Shakespeare's Hamlet.

ROBERT F. WILLSON, Jr.: Lear's Auction. JAMES N. WISE: Emerson's "Experience" and "Sons and Lovers". JAMES D. YOUNG: Aims in Reader's Theatre.

Volume 7. Amsterdam 1973 235 p. Hfl. 40.—
HANEY H. BELL Jr.: Sam Fathers and Ike McCaslin and the World in Which Ike Matures. SAMUEL IRVING BELLMAN: The Apocalypse in Literature. HALDEEN BRADDY: England and English before Alfred. DAVID R. CLARK: Robert Frost: "The Thatch" and "Directive". RALPH MAUD: Robert Crowley, Puritan Satirist. KATHARINE M. MORSBERGER: Hawthorne's "Borderland": The Locale of the Romance. ROBERT E. MORSBERGER: The Conspiracy of the Third International. "What is the metre of the dictionary?" — Dylan Thomas. RAYMOND PRESTON: Dr. Johnson and Aristotle. JOHN J. SEYDOW: The Sound of Passing Music: John Neal's Battle for American Literary Independence. JAMES H. SIMS: Enter Satan as Esau, Alone; Exit Satan as Belshazzar: *Paradise Lost*, BOOK (IV). MICHAEL WEST, Dryden and the Disintegration of Renaissance Heroic Ideals. RENATE C. WOLFF: Pamela as Myth and Dream.

Volume 8. Amsterdam 1973. 231 p. Hfl. 40.—
SAMUEL I. BELLMAN: Sleep, Pride, and Fantasy: Birth Traumas and Socio-Biologic Adaptation in the American-Jewish Novel. PETER BUITEN-HUIS: A Corresponding Fabric: The Urban World of Saul Bellow. DAVID R. CLARK: An Excursus upon the Criticism of Robert Frost's "Directive". FRANCIS GILLEN: Tennyson and the Human Norm: A Study of Hubris and Human Commitment in Three Poems by Tennyson. ROBERT R. HARSON: H. G. Wells: The Mordet Island Episode. JULIE B. KLEIN: The Art of Apology: "An Epistle to Dr. Arbuthnot" and "Verses on the Death of Dr. Swift". ROBERT E. MORSBERGER: The Movie Game in Who's Afraid of Virginia Woolf and The Boys in the Band. EDWIN MOSES: A Reading of "The Ancient Mariner". JOHN H. RANDALL: Romeo and Juliet in the New World. A Study in James, Wharton, and Fitzgerald "Fay ce que vouldras". JOHN E. SAVESON: Conrad as Moralist in Victory. ROBERT M. STROZIER: Politics, Stoicism, and the Development of Elizabethan Tragedy. LEWIS TURCO: Manoah Bodman: Poet of the Second Awakening.

Volume 9. Amsterdam 1973. 251 p. Hfl. 40.—
THOMAS E. BARDEN: Dryden's Aims in *Amphytryon*. SAMUEL IRVING BELLMAN: Marjorie Kinnan Rawling's Existentialist Nightmare *The Yearling*. SAMUEL IRVING BELLMAN: Writing Literature for Young People. Marjorie Kinnan Rawlings' "Secret River" of the Imagination. F. S. JANZOW: "Philadelphus," A New Essay by De Quincey. JACQUELINE KRUMP: Robert Browning's Palace of Art. ROBERT E. MORSBERGER: The Winning of Barbara Undershaft: Conversion by the Cannon Factory, or "Wot prawce selvytion nah?" DOUGLAS L. PETERSON: Tempest-Tossed Barks and Their Helmsmen in Several of Shakespeare's Plays. STANLEY POSS: Serial Form and Malamud's Schlemihls. SHERYL P. RUTLEDGE: Chaucer's Zodiac of Tales. CONSTANCE RUYS: John Pickering—Merchant Adventurer and Playwright. JAMES H. SIMS: Death in Poe's Poetry: Varia-

tions on a Theme. ROBERT A. SMITH: A Pioneer Black Writer and the Problems of Discrimination and Miscegenation. ALBERT J. SOLOMON: The Sound of Music in "Eveline": A Long Note on a Barrel-Organ. J. L. STYAN: Goldsmith's Comic Skills. ARLINE R. THORN: Shelley's *The Cenci* as Tragedy. E. THORN: James Joyce: Early Imitations of Structural Unity. LEWIS TURCO: The Poetry of Lewis Turco. An Interview by Gregory Fitzgerald and William Heyen.

New Series. Volume 1. Edited by James L. W. West III. Amsterdam 1974. 194 p. Hfl. 40.—
D. W. ROBERTSON, Jr.: Chaucer's Franklin and His Tale. CLARENCE H. MILLER and CARYL K. BERREY: The Structure of Integrity: The Cardinal Virtues in Donne's "Satyre III". F. SAMUEL JANZOW: The English Opium-Eater as Editor. VICTOR A. KRAMER: Premonition of Disaster: An Unpublished Section for Agee's *A Death in the Family*. GEORGE L. GECKLE: Poetic Justice and *Measure for Measure*. RODGER L. TARR: Thomas Carlyle's Growing Radicalism: The Social Context of *The French Revolution*. G. THOMAS TANSELLE: Philip Gaskell's *A New Introduction to Bibliography*. Review Essay. KATHERINE B. TROWER: Elizabeth D. Kirk's *The Dream Thought of Piers Plowman*. Review Essay. JAMES L. WEST III: Matthew J. Bruccoli's *F. Scott Fitzgerald a Descriptive Bibliography*. Review Essay. JAMES E. KIBLER: R. W. Stallman's *Stephen Crane: A Critical Bibliography*. Review. ROBERT P. MILLER: Jonathan Saville's *The Medieval Erotic Alba*. Review.

New Series. Volume 2. **THACKERY. Edited by Peter L. Shillingsburg.** Amsterdam 1974. 359 p. Hfl. 70.—
JOAN STEVENS: *Vanity Fair* and the London Skyline. JANE MÍLLGATE: History *versus* Fiction: Thackeray's Response to Macaulay. ANTHEA TRODD: Michael Angelo Titmarsh and the Knebworth Apollo. PATRICIA R. SWEENEY: Thackeray's Best Illustrator. JOAN STEVENS: Thackeray's Pictorial Capitals. ANTHONY BURTON: Thackeray's Collaborations with Cruikshank, Doyle, and Walker. JOHN SUTHERLAND: A *Vanity Fair* Mystery: The Delay in Publication. JOHN SUTHERLAND: Thackeray's Notebook for *Henry Esmond*. EDGAR F. HARDEN: The Growth of *The Virginians* as a Serial Novel: Parts 1–9. GERALD C. SORENSEN: Thackeray Texts and Bibliographical Scholarship. PETER L. SHILLINSBURG: Thackeray Texts: A Guide to Inexpensive Editions. RUTH apROBERTS: Thackeray Boom: A Review. JOSEPH E. BAKER: Reading Masterpieces in Isolation: Review. ROBERT A. COLBY and JOHN SUTHERLAND: Thackeray's Manuscripts: A Preliminary Census of Library Locations.

New Series. Volume 3. Edited by James L. W. West III. Amsterdam 1975. 184 p. Hfl. 40.—
SAMUEL J. ROGAL: Hurd's Editorial Criticism of Addison's Grammar and Usage. ROBERT P. MILLER: Constancy Humanized: Trivet's Constance and the Man of Law's Custance. WELDON THORNTON: Structure and Theme in Faulkner's *Go Down, Moses*. JAYNE K. KRIBBS: John Davis: A Man For His Time. STEPHEN E. MEATS: The Responsibilities of an Editor of Correspon-

dence. Review Essay. RODGER L. TARR: Carlyle and Dickens *or* Dickens and Carlyle. Review. CHAUNCEY WOOD: Courtly Lovers: An Unsentimental View. Review.

New Series. Volume 4. Edited by James L. W. West III. Amsterdam 1975. 179 p. Hfl. 40.—
JAMES L. W. WEST III: A Bibliographer's Interview with William Styron. J. TIMOTHY HOBBS: The Doctrine of Fair Use in the Law of Copyright. JUNE STEFFENSEN HAGEN: Tennyson's Revisions of the Last Stanza of "Audley Court". CLIFFORD CHALMERS HUFFMAN: *The Christmas Prince*: University and Popular Drama in the Age of Shakespeare. ROBERT L. OAKMAN: Textual Editing and the Computer. Review Essay. T.H. HOWARD-HILL: The Bard in Chains: *The Harvard Concordance to Shakespeare.* Review Essay. BRUCE HARKNESS: Conrad Computerized and Concordanced. Review Essay. MIRIAM J. SHILLINGSBURG: A Rose is a Four-Letter Word; or, The Machine Makes Another Concordance. Review Essay. RICHARD H. DAMMERS: Explicit Statement as Art. Review Essay. A. S. G. EDWARDS: Medieval Madness and Medieval Literature. Review Essay. NOEL POLK: Blotner's Faulkner. Review.

New Series. Volume 5—6. GYASCUTUS. Studies in Antebellum Southern Humorous and Sporting Writing. Edited by James L. W. West III. Amsterdam 1978.
NOEL POLK: The Blind Bull, Human Nature: Sut Lovingood and the Damned Human Race. HERBERT P. SHIPPEY: William Tappan Thompson as Playwright. LELAND H. COX, Jr.: Porter's Edition of *Instructions to Young Sportsmen.* ALAN GRIBBEN: Mark Twain Reads Longstreet's *Georgia Scenes.* T. B. THORPE's Far West Letters, ed. Leland H. Cox, Jr. An Unknown Tale by GEORGE WASHINGTON HARRIS ed. William Starr. JOHNSON JONES HOOPER's "The 'Frinnolygist' at Fault" ed. James L. W. West III. SOUTH CAROLINA WRITERS in the *Spirit of the Times* ed. Stephen E. Meats. A NEW MOCK SERMON ed. James L. W. West III. ANOTHER NEW MOCK SERMON ed. A. S. Wendel. The PORTER-HOOPER Correspondence ed. Edgar E. Thompson.

New Series. Volume 7. **SANFORD PINSKER: The Languages of Joseph Conrad.** Amsterdam 1978. 87 p. Hfl. 20.—
Table of Contents: Foreword. Introductory Language. The Language of the East. The Language of Narration. The Language of the Sea. The Language of Politics. *Victory* As Afterword.

New Series. Volume 8. **GARLAND CANNON: An Integrated Transformational Grammar of the English Language.** Amsterdam 1978. 315 p. Hfl. 60.—
Table of Contents: Preface. 1) A Child's Acquisition of His First Language. 2) Man's Use of Language. 3) Syntactic Component: Base Rules. 4) Syntactic Component: Lexicon. 5) Syntactic Component: Transformational Rules. 6) Semantic Component. 7) Phonological Component. 8) Man's Understanding of His Language. Appendix: the Sentence-Making Model. Bibliography. Index.

Biblical Allusion in *Paradise Lost*. *Absalom and Achitophel;* and Milton's *Paradise Lost*. Asem-Goldsmith's Solution to Timon's Dilemma. Dr. Johnson: A Modern Example of Christian Constancy. A Unifying Element in Tennyson's *Maud.* Arnold's Relevancy to the Twentieth Century. Sophocles' Role in "Dover Beach". Lest We Forget, Lest We Forget: Kipling's Warning to Humanity. The Garden Imagery in *Great Expectations.* "Victorian" Women in *Barchester Towers.* Another Look at "Youth". Forster's "The Road from Colonus". Biblical Influences in *Cry, the Beloved Country.* Huxley's *Island:* A Contemporary *Utopia.* The Generation Gap in Literature. Bred and Bawn in a Briar Patch — Deception in the Making. Success and Failure in the Poetry of Edwin Arlington Robinson. Naturalistic Tendencies in *Spoon River Anthology.* Primitiveness in "The Bravest Boat". Theme of Suffering in "Sonny's Blues". Nabokov's "First Love". The Temper of Romanticism in *Travels with Charley.* Unrecognized Artists in American Literature: Chicano Renaissance.

New Series: Volume 15. **ROBERT F. WILLSON, JR.: Landmarks of Shakespeare Criticism.** Amsterdam 1979. 113p. 25,–

Contents: Introduction. Thomas Rymer: On *Othello* (1692). Nicholas Rowe: Preface (1709-14). Alexander Pope: Preface (1725). Lewis Theobald: Preface (1740). Samuel Johnson: Preface (1765). Richard Farmer: Essay on the Learning of Shakespeare (1767). Gotthold Lessing: On Ghosts (1769). Walter Whiter: On Hell and Night in *Macbeth* (1794). William Richardson: On the Faults of Shakespeare (1797). August Wilhelm von Schlegel: Lecture XXIII. Shakespeare (1809-11). Johann Wolfgang von Goethe: Shakespeare ad Infinitum (1812?). Samuel Taylor Coleridge: On Shakespeare as a Poet (1811-12). William Hazlitt: On Shakespeare and Milton (1818). Thomas de Quincey: On the Knocking at the Gate in *Macbeth* (1823). Thomas Carlyle: The Hero as a Poet (1841). Ivan Turgenev: Hamlet and Don Quixote: the Two Eternal Human Types (1860). Edward Dowden: Shakespeare's Portraiture of Women (1888). Walter Pater: Shakespeare's English Kings (1889). Bernard ten Brink: Shakespeare as a Comic Poet (1895). Richard Moulton: Supernatural Agency in the Moral World of Shakespeare (1903). Leo Tolstoy: Shakespeare and the Drama (1906). J.J. Jusserand: What to Expect of Shakespeare (1911-12). Sigmund Freud: On Lady Macbeth (1916). George Bernard Shaw: On Cutting Shakespear (1919). Edmund Blunden: Shakespeare's Significances (1929). Selected Bibliography.

New Series: Volume 16. **A.H. Qureshi: Edinburgh Review and Poetic Truth.** Amsterdam 1979. 61p. 15,–

New Series: Volume 17. **RAYMOND J.S. GRANT: Cambridge Corpus Christi College 41: The Loricas and the Missal.** Amsterdam 1979. 127p. 30,–

Contents: Chapter I: The Loricas of Corpus 41. Chapter II: Corpus 41 — An 11th-Century English Missal. Appendix: Latin Liturgical material contained in the Margins of Cambridge, Corpus Christi College 41. Endnotes: Chapter I and Chapter II.

New Series: Volume 18. **CARLEE LIPPMAN**: Lyrical Positivism. Amsterdam 1979. 195p. 40,–
Contents: Chapter I: Some Tenets. Chapter II: The Rape of *The Rape of the Lock.* Chapter III: García Márquez' Language Laboratory. Chapter IV: The Syntax of Persuasion. Afterword. Bibliography.

New Series: Volume 19. **EVELYN A. HOVANEC: Henry James and Germany.** Amsterdam 1979. 149p. 30,–
Contents: Preface. Introduction. Chapter I: A Travel Sketch. Chapter II: The Analytic Tourist. Chapter III: Life Into Fiction. Chapter IV: Value, Inconsistency, and Resolution. Bibliography. Index.

New Series: Volume 20. **SANDY COHEN: Norman Mailer's Novels.** Amsterdam 1979. 133p. 25,–
Contents: Chapter One: Norman Mailer in Context. Chapter Two: The Naked and the Dead. Chapter Three: Barbary Shore. Chapter Four: The Deer Perk. Chapter Five: An American Dream. Chapter Six: History As Novel As History: Armies of the Night. Chapter Seven: Why Are We In Vietnam? A Novel. Chapter Eight: Marilyn. A Biographical Note.

New Series: Volume 21. **HANS BERTENS:** The Fiction of Paul Bowles. Amsterdam 1979. 260p. 50,–
Contents: Chapter One: Introduction. Chapter Two: The Sheltering Sky. Chapter Three: Let It Come Down. Chapter Four: The Spider's House. Chapter Five: Up Above the World. Chapter Six: The Stories. Chapter Seven: Conclusion. Selected Bibliography. Index.

New Series: Volume 22. **RICHARD MANLEY BLAU:** The Body Impolitic. Amsterdam 1979. 214p. 45,–
Contents: Preface. Chapter I. Typee: In Search of Plump Sphericity. Chapter II. White Jacket: To Scourge a Man that is a Roman. Chapter III. Moby-Dick: Beware of the Spinal Complaint. Chapter IV. Pierre: Let them look out for me now! Epilogue. Bibliography.

New Series: Volume 23. From Caxton to Beckett, Essays presented to W.H. Toppen on the occasion of his seventieth birthday, Edited by Jacques B.H. Alblas and Richard Todd. With a foreword by A.J. Fry. Amsterdam 1979. 133p. 30,–
Contents: List of Plates. Foreword. Acknowledgements. Hans H. Meier: Middle English Styles in Translation: A Note on *Everyman* and Caxton's *Reynard.* Richard Todd: The Passion Poems of George Herbert. Jacques B.H. Alblas: The Earliest Editions of *The Pilgrim's Progress* as Source Texts for the First Dutch Translation of Bunyan's Allegory. Peter J. de Voogd et al.: A Reading of William Hogarth's *Marriage à la Mode.* M. Buning: *Lessness* Magnified. A.J. Fry: On the Agonies of Elitism.

New Series: Volume 24. **CAROL JOHNSON**: The Disappearance of Literature. Amsterdam 1980. 123p. 25,–

Contents: Chapter One: The Disappearance of Literature. Chapter Two: Randall Jarrell and the Art of Self Defense. Chapter Three: Paul Valery: The Art of Concealment. Chapter Four: Hart Crane's Unimproved Infancy. Chapter Five: John Berryman: The Will to Exceed. Chapter Six: The Poetics of Disregard: Homage to Basil Bunting. Chapter Seven: The Translator as Poet. Chapter Eight: An Adjunct to the Poet's Dossier. Chapter Nine: The Consummation of Consciousness: The Poetry of Delmore Schwartz. Chapter Ten: Mrs. Wharton's Profession: The Reef. Reconnoitered. Chapter Eleven: Eça De Queiroz: The Arbitrations of Irony. Chapter Twelve: Nabokov's Ada: Word's End. Chapter Thirteen: Hysteria Naturalized.

New Series. Volume 25. **LINGUISTIC STUDIES offered to Berthe Siertsema**, edited by D.J. van Alkemade, A. Feitsma, W.J. Meys, P. van Reenen en J.J. Spa Amsterdam 1980. 382p. 56,–

Contents: D.J. van Alkemade: Referentiality and definiteness of NP's. D.M. Bakker: On *a*-generic sentences in Dutch. F. Balk-Smit Duyzentkunst: Metaphor and linguistic theory. R.A. Blust: Iban antonymy: a case from diachrony? S.C. Dik: On term coordination in functional grammar. A. Hurkmans: De Saussure and Wittgenstein. J.G. Kooij: Preposed PP's in Dutch and the definition of grammatical relations. P. Pitha: Case Frames of Nouns. S.R. Slings: 'KAI adversativum' – some thoughts on the semantics of coordination. E.M. Uhlenbeck: Observations in semantics is not easy. P.A. Verburg: Discipline versus philosophy. R. Botha: Allen's theory of synthetic compounding: a critical appraisal. H.H. Meier: Agnimals in English: group words in word groups. W.J. Meys: Morphemic make-up and lexical dynamics. Q.I.M. Mok: Le préfixe *RE*-re-regardé: productivité et potentialité. P. van Reenen/ J. Voorhoeve: Gender in Limbum. H. Schultink: On stacking up affixes, mainly in Dutch words. W. Zwanenburg: Regards du 17e siècle français sur la productivité morphologique. A. Cohen: The word as a processing unit in speech perception. A. Dees/ P. van Reenen: L'interprétation des graphies *-o-* et *-ou-* à la lumière des formes trouvées dans les chartes françaises du 13e siècle. H.D. Meijering: *D(e)*-deletion in the past tense of the class II weak verbs in Old Frisian. H. Mol: Gesture phonetics. J. Stewart: The feature Advanced Tongue Root and the Lepsius diacritics. J. Vachek: Writing and the glossematicists. B.P.F. Al: Sur la richesse lexicale du corpus d'Orléans. Contribution à l'analyse sociolinguistique d'un vocabulaire oral. J.T. Bendor-Samuel: Is a sociolinguistic profile necessary? A. Feitsma: The Frisian native speaker between Frisian and Dutch. G.J. Hartman: The goal-directedness of the process of sentence perception. E.A. Nida: The contribution of linguistics to the theory and practice of translating. J.J. Spa: Le langage et la sémiologie. Quelques réflexions nouvelles. B.T. Tervoort: What is the native language of a deaf child?

New Series. Volume 26. **FROM COOPER TO PHILIP ROTH**, Essays on American Literature, Presented to J.G. Riewald, on the occasion of his seventieth brithday. Edited by J. Bakker and D.R.M. Wilkinson, with a foreword by J. Gerritsen. Amsterdam 1980. 118p. 25,–

Contents: Foreword; T.A. Birrell: A Preface to Cooper's *The Last of the Mohicans*; A.J. Fry: *Writing New Englandy*: A Study of Diction and Technique in the Poetry of Emily Dickinson; D.R.M. Wilkinson: A Complete Image: James's *The Bostonians*; S. Betsky-Zweig: From Pleached Garden to Jungle and Waste Land: Henry James's Beast; J. Bakker: Faulkner's World as the Extension of Reality: *As I Lay Dying* Reconsidered; H.I. Schvey: Madonna at the Poker Night: Pictorial Elements in Tennessee Williams' *A Streetcar Named Desire;* G.A.M. Janssens: Styron's Case and "Sophie's Choice"; J.W. Bertens: "The Measured Self vs. The Insatiable Self:" Notes on Philip Roth; Curriculum Vitae; Publications; Tabula Gratulatorum.

Editions Rodopi N.V., Keizersgracht 302-304, Amsterdam, The Netherlands